Mike:

To the only salesman I know who has not been involved in FRAUD.

Best wishes + Love to my Brother

Jay

P.S. And of course my favorite neice Sarah Rose.

ACCESS DEVICE FRAUD and RELATED FINANCIAL CRIMES

Jerry Iannacci
Ron Morris

CRC Press
Boca Raton London New York Washington, D.C.

Library of Congress Cataloging-in-Publication Data

Iannaci, Jerry.
Access device fraud and related financial crimes / by Jerry Iannacci and Ron Morris
p. cm.
Includes bibliographical references and index.
ISBN 0-8493-8130-4 (alk. paper)
1. Commercial crimes. 2. Fraud. 3. Crime. 4. Forensic science.
I. Morris, Ron. II. Title.
HV6768.I2 1999
364.16′8—dc21 99-37130
CIP

Direct all inquiries to CRC Press LLC, 2000 Corporate Blvd., N.W., Boca Raton, Florida 33431.

International Standard Book Number 0-8493-8130-4
Library of Congress Card Number 99-37130
Printed in the United States of America 1 2 3 4 5 6 7 8 9 0
Printed on acid-free paper

Preface

When we were approached to write this book, several facts were considered before entering into the endeavor. First and foremost, it was an opportunity to work with some good friends and colleagues on a project. Second, it was to show our sincere dedication to this discipline.

Our inspiration has been garnered from many years of being associated with financial crimes in either a law enforcement capacity or the corporate investigative world. Through the efforts, in part, of the International Association of Financial Crimes Investigators, our task forces, and similar involvements, we have been privileged to be associated with and trained by some of the most recognized experts in the world. For this we say more than thank you and show our gratitude by sharing some of this knowledge throughout this textbook. The text is our cookbook, full of basic information. It is not designed to be a "how to" or to show you the "only" way to conduct an investigation; rather, it is intended to create an awareness of and a technical understanding for the discipline.

Financial crimes are growing daily and have directed investigators to the need for a better understanding as to the scope and impact of such crimes. The days of the few, quick investigative notes on a memo pad are gone. The year 2000 will shed new light on how the age of technology will play a major role in how criminals do business. The investigator, lawyer, and judiciary officer need to stay abreast of technology and criminal trends to understand, investigate, or adjudicate financial and related crimes.

Introduction

An informant once said to us, "Man, you have to be crazy to use a gun to hold up a bank; those credit cards can get you the same thing with no risk." Whether it be filling out fraudulent applications, stealing cards from the mail, or taking over legitimate accounts, it can be done — "You have to pick them though, watch out for the good banks; they've got systems to catch you if you don't know what you are doing. They come down on you hard, too!"

Credit card fraud or access device fraud is the first choice of many criminals in the world of financial crime. Why? Simply because the criminals are taking advantage of the fact that we are becoming a global plastic society. Consumers in the United States spend a significant amount of money on plastic each year, and, as we approach the new millennium, credit card use will more than double, as will the need for an access device to contain information for a variety of consumer uses. The computer age has allowed this initially simple device to become a conduit to the information superhighway. Whether intended for use at automated teller machines or on the Internet, this device is capable of housing a microchip with unbelievable amounts of information ... not only for the security of the card, but also to store and transmit unlimited information for business transactactions or even, for example, receiving health care benefits by its user. Hence, the organized crime market has become very interested in access devices.

How can these criminals best benefit from (and how can they beat) the financial institutions, retailers, and consumers? Our book is the culmination of frontline experience and is a reference text that will afford the student, financial investigator, or law enforcement professional true insight into this growing crime. We will cite case studies and take you to the scene of several of our already adjudicated cases. Our goal has been to make this text an ongoing reference, practical and easy to understand for the novice in the financial crime discipline. Our intent is for you to feel the intensity and magnitude of these crimes which require expert investigative skills and to understand how much patience you must have in solving this type of crime, which often involves arduous months of street work, as well as meticulous analytical evaluation. Another requirement is connections and communication with the International Association of Financial Crimes Investigators (IAFCI, formally called the IACCI), which is discussed in the text.

Access device fraud has been viewed by many until recently as a victimless crime — it is only the "big banks" or department stores who lose the money. Recent major cases have shown investigators, prosecutors, and judges what effect these crimes have on their victims. These financial crimes are far from victimless. In fact, financial crimes have proven to be direct links to organized crime, violent crimes, and drugs.

Our book will help the reader understand what it takes to be a successful investigator or prosecutor in this discipline. Financial crime statistics are staggering in our society, and, despite the vigorous efforts of law enforcement and industry, the criminal's sophistication grows by leaps and bounds.

An important section of the text includes the expertise of Ron Morris, to many a world-renowned expert in questioned documents. Ron is a veteran of the U.S. Secret Service Forensic Services Division in Washington, D.C. He has been credited internationally for creating the world's largest database of counterfeit/altered credit cards. Many law enforcement agencies and card issuers in the United States and certainly abroad have recognized him as a leading expert in this field. His tenacity and scientific ability have truly been the catalyst for successful prosecution through identification and forensic analysis of counterfeit plants and many related financial investigations.

The Authors

Jerry Iannacci is the current CEO of Catoctin Consultants in Frederick, MD. He is married to a veteran high school educator and is the father of three children. His background includes being a law enforcement officer in Long Island, NY; Director of Safety and Security Operations in Washington, D.C., for a major hotel corporation; and an executive with a major financial corporation, serving as its Deputy Director for Investigations. In this last capacity, he was assigned to the U.S. Secret Service Task Force in Washington, D.C., to help organize one of the world's most successful cooperatives between the government, public, and private sectors in the quest to reduce organized crime, particularly in the area of financial fraud. After only two years of operation, this consortium of banks, police, and federal agencies received the Attorney General's award for their successes. Iannacci has been president of the International Association of Financial Crimes Investigators (Mid-Atlantic States), in addition to being a member of the organization's National Board of Directors and serving as the Training and Education Chairperson. IAFCI represents over 4000 law enforcement and industry investigators around the globe with the intent of preventing and combating financial and related crimes. Iannacci was a special advisor to the Pentagon during the Gulf War and has lectured internationally on Task Force Cooperatives and the importance of joining forces in fighting crime and related problems. Recently, he was named as a consultant to CBS News, and he has been a guest on a number of television and radio talk shows, including National Urban Radio. A few years ago, Iannacci decided to apply his investigative experience to look at criminal activity and organized groups that involve youth. When he joined Catoctin Consultants, his goal was to help the Maryland State Police introduce before the Maryland General Assembly a bill on child pornography and Internet-related crimes, which did happen in 1998. Then, in 1999, he was requested by the Maryland Senate to help pass the Fraud Identity Takeover Act. As Catoctin Consultants' CEO, Iannacci spends a great deal of time volunteering through his latest appointment as the Western Maryland Chairperson for Communities in Schools and as a State Board of Directors member.

Ron Morris is one of the most globally recognized forensic examiners. He is married and has two children. In 1998, he retired from the U.S. Secret Service Forensic Services Division after approximately 37 years of federal government service, 26 of those years working as an Examiner of Questioned Documents. Before joining the Secret Service in 1975, he worked for the Questioned Document Laboratory of the Washington, D.C., Metropolitan Police Department, and the Examiner of Questioned Documents Office, U.S. Treasury Department, where he began his training. In 1998, after his retirement, he formed Ronald N. Morris and Associates, Inc., a forensic document consulting firm serving lawyers, government agencies, law enforcement, and INTERPOL. During his last 4 years with the Secret Service, he had served as the Chairman of the Subgroup of Experts on the INTERPOL International Counterfeit Payment Card Classification System work group. Today, he continues his service to INTERPOL as a consultant on implementation of the system developed by the work group. He has received numerous accommodations for his work with counterfeit payment cards from investigative organizations and law enforcement agencies around the world. He is the author of numerous papers and training materials on handwriting/hand-printing identification, counterfeit payment cards, and other aspects of questioned documents. He has conducted many training seminar workshops for the International Association of Financial Crimes Investigators, law enforcement officer training programs (such as the Federal Law Enforcement Training Center in Brunswick, GA), and the Secret Service Basic Agent Training Program.

Acknowledgments

This textbook is dedicated to many people. We thought it appropriate to identify each by name to acknowledge their contributions, support, and friendship over the years. Each of you has taught us in a very special way that you are only as good as those who surround you.

To our professional counterparts who advised, supported, and stood by us in the International Association of Financial Crimes Investigators, in both the Law Enforcement and Industry Sectors ... thank you!

To the men and women of law enforcement who have given their lives to make this a better world ... thank you!

To our counterparts all over the globe who have worked with us for a common good ... thank you!

To some very special friends and colleagues ... thank you! Steve Kenyon; the Law Offices of Marc S. Ward, Esq. & Associates (Sue, Mary, and Carey); Richard "Big Foot" Stine; Jim and Marilyn Greene; Patricia Thompson; Catoctin Consultants; Russ and Carol Meltzer; Renee and Don Woolard; Eve and Bud O'Brien; Chief and Mrs. Joseph Loeffler; Chief and Mrs. Edward Paradiso; Alan Castellana; Rin and Susan Musser; Michael Keskin; Rodney and Carla Bayton; Jimmy Gaughran; 1993 Charter Members of the Metro-Alien Fraud Task Force; Bill Burch; SAIC; Kenny LeMaster; Courtney Wheeler; Chuck Baggeroer; Det. Constable Phil Harris, U.K.; Bob Cannon; Commander Miguel Herraiz, Royal Guard, Spain; Rich Rhode; Louis Mealetti; colleagues of the Interpol counterfeit payment card classification work group; the Forensic Services division of the U.S. Secret Service, Washington, D.C.; and to our associates at the various payment card and manufacturing industries.

Table of Contents

Dedication

Jerry Iannacci

It is difficult to articulate in a few simple words an expression of dedication. First and foremost, I must dedicate this book to my grandparents Rose and Vincent Yannacci. Their spirit and love remain part of my life and have often helped me through many of life's challenges.

Of course, I dedicate this book also to my wife, Angie ... thanks for being there!

To my children, Nina, Christopher, and Anthony; Mom and Dad; Joe and Mike; Amy; and Mom and Dad P. ... Love you all!

To our technical associate author, Charles F. Baggeroer (Chuck) ... thank you for all your research and personal knowledge; your contribution to Chapter 7 was invaluable.

To Ron ... thanks for standing by me; your almost 16 years of advice, support, and trust remind me always of the importance of friendship and faith.

Ron Morris

I would like to dedicate this book to my wife, Mary, for her understanding when I would walk around with something on my mind and then just disappear into my office to write.

To Jerry ... thanks for allowing me the opportunity to contribute to this work and for allowing Angie to help me review and edit.

To Detective Constable Philip Harris, of the West Midlands Police Fraud Squad, U.K. ... for your research and contributions to U.K. law statutes.

To the Federal Bureau of Investigation, Washington, D.C., for research assistance with the fingerprint section, as well as providing specimens.

To Dennis Brosan, Visa International, Virginia.

To those who remain silent contributors ... our thanks!

I would also like to dedicate this book to all of the investigators and payment card industry people who helped me over the years. Without their assistance it would not have been possible for us to accomplish what we did and make the entire law enforcement community aware of how forensics can be of assistance to them in payment card cases.

Chapters 1–10

The History of Access Devices

1

People use credit cards and other such devices to manage money and avoid carrying large sums of cash. The access device, or credit card, has evolved tremendously since after World War II. These devices are nothing more than a convenient vehicle to transact business, maintain data, or even make a phone call. The technology is not limited to payment devices, as it is also used with security access cards, which are used to gain secure or controlled access to a building or hotel. Initially, when cards of this nature were designed, they were very basic and bore minimum standards of protection against unauthorized or illegal use. Today, the access device or credit card has evolved to be a champion of technology. It not only reflects the specific product or customer its serves, but it also has the ability to store and maintain several levels of data and security. These levels include specialized encryption, biometrics, and the latest technology utilizing integrated circuits, also known as IC or Smart Cards. Yes, the technology age has taken this rather simple device and given it the capabilities to foil many a thief or counterfeiter. We no longer are using a device that simply reflects a retailer's name, a card number, or merchant bank.

This device has evolved in part as a pro-active movement to stay ahead of potential fraud and other related crimes against such a product and its issuers. The criminal has viewed this crime as victimless and offering little face-to-face risks. For example, why enter a bank and commit a robbery, when you can achieve nearly the same result, if not better, by attempting credit card fraud? However, it is not as easy as it sounds. What this particular criminal might not count on is the level of security now very evident in cards and related products in the technology age. A credit card or telephone card is not as easy to counterfeit as it was during this product's infancy; both the device itself and its related transactions or access can be systematically traced, often within minutes of its use. Be assured that such monitoring is very much the case with a diligent issuer whose main concern is his customer or authorized user. Excellent systematic recordkeeping at the touch of a keyboard has given investigators up-to-the-minute access to transaction history as well as location of use.

Examples of Types of Access Devices

Bank or Financial Credit Cards

Examples of these cards include Visa, MasterCard, American Express, JCB, Diner's Club, and Discover, to name a few. These devices are usually made of plastic and are about 3.5 inches long to fit conveniently in most wallets. The device has been designed to replace cash transactions by providing immediate purchasing power with an established line of credit. Such a device is recognized (with minor exceptions) worldwide, hence avoiding the need for a point-of-sale currency exchange. In other words, you can use it worldwide wherever it is recognized and purchase any goods or services offered without the need for currency. Needless to say, this is very helpful when traveling or conducting business. The purchases and exchange rates are all handled via the issuer, merchant bank, and governing association, such as Visa, MasterCard, or American Express. The accounting aspect of the process is managed systematically, and the consumer is billed monthly for purchases made against the previously established credit limit. Individual consumers as well as businesses have found this process to be an excellent method of accounting and controlling spending. This rule does not apply to all, however, as credit abuse and overspending are the addictions of those who abuse the privilege.

Retail Cards

Department store and automotive gas cards are the bulk of retail cards issued in the world economy today. Retail cards started out as being quite generic, and they were considered the thing to have to establish credit. When they first were issued, their individual use was greater than it is now, in 1999. Several factors for their reduced usage have been identified. For example, issuers have been unable to compete with annual interest rates against large issuers such as Visa, MasterCard, and American Express. Retail stores have also been forced to allow their customers to use almost all major brand cards vs. their own proprietary card. Current research suggests that this has had a negative effect on certain businesses and their solvency. In late 1998, this effect has raised certain concerns in the U.S. Department of Justice. It has been alleged that the credit card associations have had too much of a controlling factor in the marketplace and have not allowed for fair competition.

Telephone Cards

The communications industry was the latecomer to the credit card market place. AT&T, Sprint, and MCI, to name a few, found it quite advantageous to allow consumers to use such a device for their communications needs. Cards activated by simply using a telephone and PIN number (personal identification number) offer yet another alternative to carrying cash. The card is authenticated when an authorized user making a telephone call from either a pay phone or regular phone dials an access number before placing their call. The charges are then transferred to the user's account and billed monthly. In 1996, the communications industry came out with another type of access device, the telephone card. This device is transferable and is paid for in advance. Virtually no risk exists for the issuers, as they have been paid in advance for the authorized minutes on the telephone cards.

Smart Cards or Integrated Circuit Cards

This device represents one of the highest levels of security and technological advances in the marketplace today. In 1999, the card is still being integrated in the United States, while France seems to be the leader in its use, with acceptance in the European market expanding daily. The primary purpose of the Smart Card is to improve the security of using such a card, which is accomplished through embedding a microchip in the card. Another use for such a device has been to store more information on the device for various uses. Potential fraud is expected to be lower than that for conventional cards which are used in most parts of the world today. The Smart Card helps foil counterfeiters, as it is neither very cost effective nor easy to counterfeit the device. Chuck Baggeroer, one of the nation's leading experts on integrated circuit cards, contributed to our discussion of this technology in Chapter 7.

How Today's Technology Has Helped Foil Criminals

In light of the technological advances in access devices, the information that access devices store or transmit has been pivotal in major investigations, from murders to Internet crimes, as well as credit card fraud. A 1994 case in Frederick County, MD, was solved due to the efforts of law enforcement and bank investigators which led to the capture of a suspect who was charged with killing his parents and stealing their money and credit cards. He fled the state but was tracked within days after making the terrible mistake of leaving the electronic fingerprint of credit card use. Within a week of the killings, the suspect, under electronic and on-line surveillance, was detected checking into an Alabama hotel. Within one hour, swift action by local authorities and the bank investigators led to his capture and later extradition. Crimes such as these are not what a jurisdiction wants to deal with. According to bank investigator Steve Kenyon, assigned to the U.S. Secret Service Fraud Task Force, "These heinous type crimes are not only a shock to the community, but an invasion of one's entire life. If it were not for the access device use and swift and professional investigative tactics, this crime might have gone unsolved for some time." In this particular case, it was amazing to discover how the electronic fingerprint could be tracked with such surgical precision.

We are not certain what other methods could have been used to solve this crime as quickly as did the joint efforts of the bank investigator units, law enforcement, and all those assigned to the U.S. Secret Service Task Force who worked with the Frederick County Sheriff's Department to bring this suspect to justice. Their efforts resulted in a conviction in April 1999.

Much of the credit for such technological advances is due in part to the efforts of credit card associations such as Visa, MasterCard, and American Express. Certainly, technology companies such as Schlumberger Malco and Data Card International are but a few of the pioneers fostering technological advances and secure operating systems.

Parties Who Investigate — Industry and Law Enforcement

Improving security in the credit card industry is greatly supported by many law enforcement agencies in their attempts to prevent illegal use and victimization. In addition to local law enforcement, a few other key agencies are involved in this quest, such as the U.S. Postal Inspection Service and the U.S. Secret Service, which was granted primary jurisdiction of such investigations by the U.S. Congress in 1984. This extremely active industry is also supported by the efforts of the International Association of Financial Crimes Investigators, made up of over 4000 industry and law enforcement entities. Other subcommittees and focal groups now in effect include the U.S. Postal Inspection Service Quarterly Forum. These measures and pro-active approaches attest to how much impact this device has on our economy.

Significance of Access Devices in World Economy

Running a business, a country, or a global economy is contingent upon the financial solvency of any venue. To understand access devices or credit cards, you need to understand the evolution of payment devices and what effect they have on the global economy. Most of us do not relate early civilizations and their methods of payment to those of today, as we have come a long way from trading fancy stones and possessions.

In the United States, the primary form of payment is the U.S. note, or currency, sometimes referred to as the "greenback". This traditional payment device is very recognizable around the world as being U.S. currency. The first series of this note was issued in 1861, and today the uniqueness and integrity of the currency, achieved through the use of fine cotton/linen paper, green ink, and fine-line design, are yet other examples of how payment devices have evolved. The U.S. currency is in its fourth generation and has undergone many changes to assure its integrity, value, and worldwide recognition (see Chapter 3). It is quite a different story for notes or currency of other nations. They simply are not as immediately recognizable by their appearance, denomination, or value, although it is hoped that the Euro, currently being introduced in Europe, will be the exception. Former U.S. Treasury Secretary Rubin is quoted from a documentary about "knowing your money" as saying (and we paraphrase) that the United States note will always be honored, no matter its age or condition, and will maintain its value as guaranteed by the U.S. Treasury. This high level of recognition is of importance to the issuers of credit cards, as well, as long as merchants and consumers use them lawfully and in accordance with association rules and guidelines and the law. Clearly, if a consumer charges a good or service with the device, the issuer has pledged to make payment to the merchant or provider, providing the account is open and active.

The global impact of credit cards is not limited to the financial consideration of solvency. Credit-card crime is a major threat to our economy because of its attraction to criminal elements ranging from those committing simple fraud crimes to major organized crime activity. Criminal groups have no border concerns, in their minds. They seek opportunity and prey on whatever is most accessible. Such organized groups travel from state to state and country to country. They do this in an often-futile attempt to evade detection and/or prosecution. The key to combating such activity has been the pro-active response by the international law enforcement and industrial communities to work together to share intelligence on major organized crime groups and key figures. This has been the primary approach in keeping such crime down to a manageable level. Law enforcement officials and industry investigators have used the global network of the International Association of Financial Crimes Investigators to facilitate this quest, but this is only one example of the resources available to assure productive networking internationally.

History of Use of False Identification

2

The use of false identification is not a new problem. The annals of criminal law throughout the world and over many years are filled with instances of the use of fraudulent identification documents to assist in carrying out criminal conduct. In November 1974, Attorney General William Saxbe established a Federal Advisory Committee on False Identification (FACFI) to study the scope of the criminal use of false identification and to recommend actions to suppress such use. FACFI consisted of individuals from federal, state, and local governments, as well as representatives from business and various interest groups. This Committee concluded that "false identification documents could be obtained readily and inexpensively throughout the United States from a variety of commercial sources, and that genuine government identification documents could be easily obtained from the issuing offices by means of simple misrepresentations."[1]

While subsequent, enhanced legislation from federal and state legislatures has helped to combat the possession, transfer, and manufacture of false identification documents, these criminal activities continue. Indeed, most experts state that these acts are on the rise. The most prominent factor is the increased access to advanced technology by the masses which has allowed the relatively unskilled, common individual to produce high-quality identification documents inexpensively that until the last few years could only have been made by master counterfeiters. With readily available personal computers, scanners, facsimile machines, Internet access, graphics software, and other technological paraphernalia, the ability to produce quality documents of all sorts is within reach of an ever-increasing number of the public. The increased use of false identification appears to be well documented in government reports[2] and newspapers.[3] According to a recent article in the *Washington Post*:[4]

Due to the increase availability and use of advanced technology, the counterfeiting of documents used to commit crimes or facilitate criminal activity is increasing. There has been an increase in the use of false passports, drivers' licensees, birth certificates and other identification documents. Such documents are used to create a false identity, facilitating illegal immigration, fraud, as well as other criminal activity.

How False Identification Is Obtained

False identification is obtained from myriad sources. The methods and means of procuring false identification are quite varied, indeed. Many people acquire false identification on their own. They alter or manufacture it. They steal it. They make false application to unwitting issuers. Frequently, other individuals knowingly provide assistance to individuals desiring to obtain false identification. With the ever-increasing number of readily available personal computers, there has been an explosion of forgery activity of all sorts, including the manufacture of false identification.

Many people make their own false identification. Sometimes they experiment by themselves to create new documents, and sometimes they just alter an otherwise genuine document. Often they receive assistance in their individual endeavors via "underground" manuals easily obtainable through the mail or via the Internet. Individuals often steal another person's identification documents either by pick-pocketing them or through a simple larceny of unattended personal items, perhaps in a gym locker.

More often, however, individuals use the services of third parties to obtain false identification. At times, the third-party suppliers of documentation are simply performing their legitimate job, unaware of the inappropriate intentions of the acquirer. Such is the case when an individual provides false information to an issuer, such as an employer, government agency, or other institution, under circumstances in which the issuer is totally unaware of the fraudulent intentions of the person applying for the identification.

The methods used to obtain the services of false identification manufacturers are many. There may be a chance or planned encounter on a college campus with a student entrepreneur. Some individuals send away to a mail-order companies, while others go to urban downtown locations such as 42nd Street in New York City or Los Angeles, where it is not difficult to rendezvous with criminals eager to provide false identification for the right price. There are many street corners and other meeting places throughout the world where false identification may be procured.

Issuance of false identification on genuine stock, paper or plastic, by corrupt insiders is particularly problematic. Generally, the most valuable source for obtaining such false identification is a corrupt government official who can issue it in the individual's own name or someone else's. This false identification is often obtained through the bribery of government officials in various government agencies, such as state motor vehicle departments, passport offices, and the Social Security

Administration. Once identification is obtained in this manner, no amount of scrutiny by a law enforcement officer, bank clerk, or store manager can detect the fraudulent presentation, as that document was issued by the appropriate authority, albeit in an unauthorized manner. Arrests of government officials in regard to the unauthorized issuance of false identification are regularly made throughout this country and throughout the world.

In October 1989, seven people, including four State Department employees, were arrested for taking part in a conspiracy to sell nearly 300 fraudulently issued U.S. passports for amounts ranging from $5000 to $25,000 each. In December 1991, in just one case, 40 then current and former employees of the Department of Motor Vehicles were charged with trafficking in false identification documents. These employees were arrested for accepting bribes to produce and transfer fraudulent driver's licenses, registrations, learner's permits, and other DMV documents. In 1996, in another case, 20 individuals, 10 of whom were current or former employees of the Social Security Administration, were arrested in a scheme in which they released personal identification information which permitted other individuals to engage in various types of credit card fraud. All the arrests in the three cases highlighted above were conducted in one major city in the United States. Nevertheless, newspapers throughout the United States, and perhaps the world, often report the arrest of a government employee who has breached his trust by providing unauthorized identity documents.

An internal breach of any government office where identification documents are issued is a serious matter which tends to undermine the integrity of those identification documents. A corrupt employee within the Social Security administration is particularly troublesome for businesses and the government of United States because of the specific personal information readily available on nearly all Americans. This information is truly a treasure trove for individuals with criminal intent.

Among the many pieces of information contained in these files are the maiden names of individuals' mothers. This information is utilized by many financial institutions as a security measure. To verify identity over the telephone, financial institutions often request customers to recite the maiden names of their mothers. Today, it is common practice for credit card companies to send their credit cards through the mails inactivated and to require recitation of the mother's maiden name over the telephone for activation. This security measure is totally defeated when the criminal is able to acquire this information. Consequently, a corrupt Social Security employee is a valuable asset to a financial fraud operation.

How False Identification Is Utilized

There would appear to be few legitimate purposes for the use of false identification; however, federal law specifically permits use of false identification for *bona fide* law enforcement and intelligence purposes.[5] This would permit police and government agents to use false identification in undercover operations and for other lawful government purposes.

Individuals may use false identification for any number of reasons, but most uses involve criminal activity. False identification has been described as a criminal's best friend. It permits criminals to disappear by assuming the identity of another individual or even perhaps assuming the identity of a totally fictitious "paper" person. Often a person whose identity has been "borrowed" is forever unaware of his newly acquired criminal or debtor status, but sometimes it does not take so long. He may learn of his status as a result of an unmerited arrest by law enforcement, with an undeserved notification of suspended driving privileges, or with an unjustified refusal of credit.

False identification is most often used to engage in criminal activity, fraud against businesses and the government, and other prohibited conduct. The criminal use of false identification is a tremendous international problem. Within the United States alone, there is a multi-billion dollar impact on government, business, and the public. In the *Federal Identification Fraud* report issued by the Senate Permanent Subcommittee on Investigations in May 1983, the economic impact on government and commerce was estimated to be $24 billion annually because of false identification fraud. Among the many illegitimate uses of false identification are

- Smuggling operations of all sorts, including drugs and aliens
- Evading detection as a fugitive or illegal alien
- Espionage
- Terrorism (both international and domestic)
- Illegal purchase of weapons and explosives (by convicted felons and others)
- Entitlement fraud (Welfare, Medicare, Supplemental Social Security)
- Tax fraud
- Employment fraud
- Bank fraud, including check forgery, negotiating false obligations, and obtaining credit under false pretenses
- Subscription fraud in regard to many services such as cellular telephones
- Car rentals and fraudulent purchases of all sorts
- Insurance fraud of all sorts
- Underage drinking

The use of false identification in regard to diverse smuggling operations, especially those involving drugs and aliens, is rampant throughout the world. Because smuggling often carries substantial criminal penalties, those criminals engaged in such conduct strongly desire to avoid detection. Once such means is to utilize fraudulent identification documents. These documents are obtained in many different ways. They are procured through corrupt government officials, or they are purchased from the actual owners who later claim that they were lost or stolen. They may be falsely presented actual documents on loan from friends, relatives, associates, and others, while many are simply bogus documents of varying quality. Smuggling operations are very lucrative criminal enterprises. The wealth of drug traffickers, such as the Medellin and Cali cartels, is well known. Perhaps, less well known is the current multi-billion dollar trade in smuggling illegal aliens all over the globe, especially to prime destinations such as Canada, the United States, and Germany. Experts in the United States and abroad claim that the illegal monetary gains from smuggling people across borders is matching the lucrative illegal narcotics trade. In recognition of the increasing alien smuggling problem, the budget of the U.S. Immigration and Naturalization Service (the agency responsible for enforcement in this area) has been increased 72% to $3.5 billion in the 3 years following 1993. In 1995, President Clinton, in an effort to combat this growing problem, appointed a task force composed of INS, FBI, CIA, and DEA officials.

On August 20, 1996, Spanish authorities in Barcelona arrested a Mafia boss, Giuseppe Carnovale, who was in possession of false identification at the time of his arrest and was wanted for murder, arms and drug trafficking, and money laundering.[6] On September 26, 1996, near Vancouver, Canada, the Royal Canadian Mounted Police arrested Nicholas Sand, who was the alleged mastermind behind a massive illegal drug laboratory and had been a U.S. fugitive for 20 years, relying upon false identification to remain so.[7]

Many fugitives obtain false identification to avoid detection. Their motive to avoid incarceration is obvious. James Earl Ray, Patty Hearst, or Ted Bundy and countless other notorious fugitives used false identification. Often, when fugitives are finally captured they are in possession of bogus identification. The 1982 House of Representatives Report No. 97-802 entitled *False Identification Crime Control Act of 1982* states that, "A random survey of fugitives by the FBI found that all of them used false identification and that some of them had more than 30 identities."

Espionage and terrorism are two areas of criminal enterprise where very high-quality fraudulent identification documents are often utilized. Because sovereign countries often support these actions, it should not be surprising that the quality of documents used in regard to such activities would be quite good. In 1996, a terrorist was convicted in federal district court in New York on various terrorist charges, including a charge of false documents, in regard to the explosion at the World Trade Center.

Convicted felons are prohibited under federal law (18 USC) from possessing or purchasing weapons. In order to acquire weapons, such individuals have been known to utilize false identification. Also, to avoid notice by government agencies, sometimes a convicted felon will ask a confederate with no criminal record to use false identification to purchase a weapon.

The amount of entitlement fraud in the United States is tremendously large — in the billions of dollars. The use of fraudulent identification plays a significant role in these substantial losses involving public funds. Often, uninsured individuals obtain coverage through the use of false identification. The third edition of the *Social Security Number Fraud Investigative Guide*, released in March 1994 by the Department of Health and Human Services, lists various types of Social Security number (SSN) fraud:

- Using multiple false SSNs to receive various types of benefits under fictitious identities
- Using another person's name and SSN to receive benefits on that person's record

- Using a false SSN to receive medical benefits
- Working under a false SSN to conceal income while receiving disability insurance benefits, supplemental security income, or welfare benefits
- Using a false SSN to conceal receipt of veterans benefits
- Using a false SSN to file fraudulent requests for tax refunds
- Using a false SSN to obtain a refund under a state program which helps low-income elderly and disabled retain private housing
- Using a false SSN to obtain food stamps, unemployment compensation, workers' compensation benefits, and federally guaranteed student loans illegally

Losses to our state governments are also very large. In just one month, May 1996, the State of New Jersey was billed $3.5 million for nonexistent psychological services. In that case, a psychologist pleaded guilty to conspiring with more than 200 people to defraud 36 insurers.

Use of fraudulent documents hurts businesses the most. The losses to the American economy are staggering. These businesses must ultimately defray these costs with higher prices for goods and services passed on to consumers. In order to combat fraud, businesses must bear expenses in order to protect themselves, including:

- Additional salaries for security personnel
- Costs of security devices such as surveillance cameras and alarms
- Implementation of computer audit programs
- Utilization of anti-theft devices
- A cornucopia of other costly actions which add to the cost of doing business

Banks and financial institutions are hurt through schemes involving check forgery, false loans, insufficient funds, spurious financial obligations, and credit and debit cards. These schemes are discussed in detail in other sections of this book.

Businesses of all sorts, both large and small, suffer tremendous losses as the result of granting credit based on false identification. Often the identity of an individual with good credit is assumed by another possessing *animus farundi*. Businesses often have lost their leased or consigned property after presentation of false identification by the lessor or consignee. Theft of services for electricity and cellular fraud has often been conducted through the unauthorized use of the identification documents of another.

Insurance frauds of various sorts are conducted utilizing false identification. One person might receive medical benefits under another person's insurance. One seemingly healthy person might apply for life insurance in the name of another person who is not so healthy. The potential fraudulent schemes are virtually unlimited, and the attendant losses are staggering.

The desire by young people to imbibe and overcome the scrutiny of bartenders and liquor salespersons has helped to fuel a booming industry on and near college campuses. In a number of cases, this has resulted in the loss of the lives of inebriated underage drinkers or their victims. Obviously, the loss to society directly attributable to false identification in such instances is tremendous. The extent of this illicit conduct by college students was described in the 1995 testimony of Congressman Albert R. Wynn:

> *The use and manufacture of false identifications have become a growing problem for many local enforcement officials and have become a cottage industry on college campuses throughout the country. On many campuses, the manufacture and sale of fake IDs have become entrepreneurial ventures. ...In 1993, a Georgetown University student was arrested and charged with making fake IDs and mailing them to hundreds of college-aged students. It was reported that in just three months, he made nearly $30,000.*
>
> *In 1994, a George Washington University student pleaded guilty to manufacturing and mailing fake identifications to thousands of underage students in several states. In 1995, in Washington, D.C., a 16- and 22-year-old were charged with 40 counts of manufacturing fake identifications. At the raid, authorities seized $40,000 worth of computers and graphics equipment, blank driver's licenses, and several hundred order forms for licenses from the District of Columbia, Maryland, Virginia, and New Jersey. According to officials, the two gentlemen said they made $15,000 a week selling the fake licenses.*

Criminal Violations Involving False Identification (Federal and State)

There are numerous laws, both state and federal, that proscribe the fraudulent manufacture, transfer, and possession of false identification documents. The most prominent of these statutes is found in Title 18 USC Section 1028 and is entitled *Fraud and Related Activity in Connection with Identification Documents.* This statute has a very wide reach, providing coverage under specified circumstances to government identification documents of federal, state, and local governments, as well as foreign governments and international quasi-governmental organizations. Note that the coverage of 18 USC deals only with governmental identification documents.

Another important federal criminal statute is found in Title 18 USC Section 1738 and is entitled *Mailing Private Identification Documents without a Disclaimer.* This section deals with private identification documents that are sent through the mails. These two sections will be discussed in detail later.

There are many other federal statutes that deal directly and indirectly with false identification documents. Most of these statutes involve the fraudulent use, possession, counterfeiting, and forgery of specific federal documents:

- 18 USC 1306 (fraudulent application for alien registration card)
- 18 USC 499 (counterfeiting, forging, or altering military pass or permit or using or possessing such with intent to defraud)
- 18 USC 506 (forging, altering the seal of a U.S. agency, or possessing such with fraudulent intent)

- 18 USC 701 (unauthorized manufacturing, selling, or possessing identification cards used by U.S. agencies or imitations thereof)
- 18 USC 922 (furnishing false identification to acquire a firearm or ammunition)
- 18 USC 1423 (use of unlawfully obtained evidence of citizenship or naturalization)
- 18 USC 1426 (counterfeiting or selling naturalization or citizenship papers or equipment to produce certificates)
- 18 USC 1543 (forging, counterfeiting, or altering a passport or using such a passport)
- 49 USC 1472 (forging, counterfeiting, or altering aircraft certificates)

Notes

1. See *False Identification Crime Control Act of 1982,* Report No. 97-802, House of Representatives, 97th Congress, 2nd Session. This report provides background on the U.S. Federal Advisory Committee on False Identification (FACFI), findings of the FACFI Committee concerning the widespread use of false identification documents in varied criminal activity, and section-by-section analysis of then-proposed federal legislation later enacted in 18 USC 1028.
2. See Testimony of the Honorable Albert R. Wynn (D-MD) Before the House Judicial Committee Subcommittee on Crime on H.R. 1552, The False Identification Act of 1995; also, Inspector General Report in 1991 entitled *Youth and Alcohol: Laws and Enforcement.*
3. Counterfeit IDs get a high-tech face lift: computer copies stump police, bartenders, *Washington Post,* Nov. 12, 1996, Metro Section p. 8; Forgers with fake IDs leave victims reeling, *Cincinnati Enquirer,* Feb. 2, 1996, Metro Section, p. C1.
4. See Criminal Intelligence Service Canada's *Annual Report on Organized Crime,* 1996. (The report is retrievable free over the Internet at www.cisc.gc.ca/compute1.html.)
5. See Title 18, U.S. Code Section 1028(3), which states: "This section does not prohibit any lawfully authorized investigative, protective, or intelligence activity of a law enforcement agency of the United States, a State, or a subdivision of a State, or of an intelligence agency of the United States, or any activity authorized under Title V of the Organized Crime Control Act of 1970…"
6. Associated Press Worldstream, Mafia boss arrested, *International News,* Aug. 20, 1996.
7. Accused LSD lab mastermind was drug figure in '60s, *The Vancouver Sun,* Dec. 14, 1996, p. A14.

The History of Currency

3

Payment devices have come a long way in the history of the world. Money, notes, coins, and other such methods of payment have certainly seen their share of change over the years. From early time, man has used some sort of method of payment to transact business. One would think that bartering, trading, and like methods of transacting such business would be very cumbersome and difficult. In earlier civilizations, some of those transactions involved real property ranging from animals to precious goods, requiring keeping on hand or even carrying large and heavy amounts of precious metals or stones. We would have thought that paper money and coins were an innovation that would last forever. Who would have ever predicted that this advancement might one day be eliminated?

Today, as we approach the new millennium, money moves across the globe in a matter of seconds by the touch of a keyboard on a computer. The electronic commerce age has allowed us to recognize and be kept abreast of world economies and the value of various currencies as we transact business in the government, corporate, and private sectors internationally. To give you, the reader, a better understanding of the evolution of currency, we will now provide a history of the United States currency, simply because it is the most recognized payment note in the world.

A Brief Timeline of U.S. Currency

1690: Colonial Notes

In the early days of this nation, before and just after the American Revolution, Americans used English, Spanish, and French currencies. The Massachusetts Bay

Colony issued the first paper money in the colonies that would later form the United States.

1775: Continental Currency

American colonists issued paper currency for the Continental Congress to finance the Revolutionary War. The notes were backed by the "anticipation" of tax revenues. Without solid backing and easily counterfeited, the notes quickly became devalued, giving rise to the phrase "not worth a Continental."

1781: Nation's First Bank

The Continental Congress chartered the Bank of North America in Philadelphia as the nation's first "real" bank to give further support to the Revolutionary War.

1785: The Dollar

The Continental Congress adopted the dollar as the unit for national currency. At that time, private bank note companies printed a variety of notes.

1789: First Bank of the United States

After adoption of the Constitution in 1789, Congress charted the First Bank of the United States until 1881 and authorized it to issue paper bank notes to eliminate confusion and simplify trade. The bank served as the U.S. Treasury's fiscal agent, thus performing the first central bank functions.

1793: U.S. Mint

The federal monetary system was established with the creation of the U.S. Mint in Philadelphia. The first American coins were struck in 1793.

1816: Second Bank of the United States

The Second Bank of the United States was charted for 20 years, until 1836.

1836: State Bank Notes

With minimum regulation, a proliferation of 1600 state-chartered, private banks issued paper money. State bank notes, with over 30,000 variations in color and design, were easily counterfeited. Such counterfeiting, along with bank failures, caused confusion and circulation problems.

1861: Civil War

On the brink of bankruptcy and pressed to finance the Civil War, Congress authorized the U.S. Treasury to issue paper money for the first time in the form of non-interest-bearing Treasury Notes called Demand Notes.

1862: Greenbacks

United States Notes replaced Demand Notes. They were commonly called "greenbacks" and were last issued in 1971. The Secretary of the Treasury was empowered by Congress to have notes engraved and printed by private bank note companies. The notes were signed and affixed with seals by six Treasury Department employees.

1863: The Design

The design of U.S. currency incorporated a Treasury seal, the fine-line engraving necessary for the difficult-to-counterfeit intaglio printing, intricate geometric lathe-work patterns, and distinctive cotton and linen paper with embedded red and blue fibers.

1865: Gold Certificates

Gold certificates were issued by the Department of the Treasury against gold coin and bullion deposits and were circulated until 1933.

1865: Secret Service

The Department of the Treasury established the U.S. Secret Service to control counterfeiting. At that time, counterfeits were estimated to be one third of all circulation currency.

1866: National Bank Notes

National bank notes, backed by U.S. government securities, became predominant. By this time, nationally charted banks held 75% of bank deposits. As state bank notes were replaced, the value of currency stabilized for a time.

1877: Bureau of Engraving and Printing

The Department of the Treasury's Bureau of Engraving and Printing started printing all U.S. currency.

1878: Silver Certificates

The Department of the Treasury was authorized to issue silver certificates in exchange for silver dollars. The last issue was in the Series 1957.

1913: Federal Reserve Act

After the 1893 and 1907 financial panics, the Federal Reserve Act of 1913 was passed. It created the Federal Reserve System as the nation's central bank to regulate the flow of money and credit for economic stability and growth. The System was authorized to issue Federal Reserve notes, now the only U.S. currency produced and representing 99% of all currency in circulation.

1929: Standardized Design

Currency was reduced in size by 25% and featured uniform portraits on the front with emblems and monuments on the back.

1957: "In God We Trust"

Paper currency was first issued with "In God We Trust" in 1957. The inscription appears on all currency Series 1963 and later.

1990: Security Thread and Microprinting

A security thread and microprinting were introduced to deter counterfeiting by advanced copiers and printers. The features first appeared in Series 1990 $100, $50, and the $20 notes. By Series 1993, the features appeared in all denominations except $1 notes.

1994: Currency Redesign

The Secretary of the Treasury announced that U.S. currency would be redesigned to incorporate a new series of counterfeit deterrents. The newly designed $20 were issued in 1998; the new $50, in 1997; and the new $100, in 1996. The new $50 was the first to incorporate a low-vision feature.

Miscellaneous Facts about the U.S. Secret Service and Counterfeiting

- The United States issued its first national currency notes in 1861. By the end of the Civil War, counterfeits were estimated to be one third of all circulated currency. Created by the U.S. Department of the Treasury, the Secret Service had the sole mission of suppressing counterfeit currency. In less than a decade, counterfeiting was sharply reduced.
- To stem counterfeiting, the Secret Service works in conjunction with local, state, federal, and foreign law enforcement agencies. The Secret Service also maintains close working relationships with the Federal Reserve banks and domestic as well as international commercial banking institutions.
- During fiscal year 1997, a total of $136,205,241 in counterfeit U.S. currency appeared worldwide. Of this amount, 75%, or $101,516,212, was seized prior to circulation with no loss to the public.
- Production methods used in counterfeiting operations have evolved over the years, from the traditional method of offset printing to the use of color copiers and, more recently, scanners, computers, and inkjet printers.
- In the U.S., the most counterfeited denomination is the $20 note, followed by the $100 note, $10 note, $50 note, $1 note, and $5 note. The $100 note is the most common foreign-produced counterfeit note.

- To aid in counterfeit investigations, agents use the Service's modern, well-equipped Forensic Services Laboratory, which includes a complete library of specimen notes dating back to 1865, the largest watermark file and ink library in existence, and equipment to examine and analyze notes counterfeited by various types of printing methods and office machine copiers.
- During fiscal year 1997, the disposition of arrests showed a 98.9% conviction rate for counterfeiting cases. The Secret Service is committed to a zero tolerance policy and is determined to investigate each and every counterfeiting case. Each case, no matter how large or small, carries the serious consequences of incarceration and/or fines.

History of the New Series

Until the late 1920s, U.S. currency was redesigned frequently, and there were several types of notes in circulation: U.S. notes, national bank notes, and silver certificates. Since the introduction of the Series 1928 Federal Reserve notes, changes in the design have not affected the overall architecture of U.S. currency. This includes the use of microprinting and security threads in Series 1990 and later notes. The counterfeit-deterrent features added in Series 1990 were the first step in responding to advances in reprographic technologies. Although these features have proved effect and will be retained, additional measures are necessary to protect U.S. currency against future threats posed by continued improvements in copy machines, scanners, and printers. The new design, beginning with Series 1996, is the culmination of a 5-year study aimed at staying ahead of the counterfeiting threat and is part of a continuing process to protect U.S. currency. At the same time, the redesign process has provided an opportunity to incorporate features that will make U.S. currency more readily identifiable, especially by the low-vision community.

The process began with the New Currency Design Task Force, which was made up of representatives of the U.S. Treasury Department, Federal Reserve System, U.S. Secret Service, and the Bureau of Engraving and Printing (BEP). The Task Force made its recommendations to the Advanced Counterfeit Deterrence Steering Committee, also composed of representatives of the Treasury Department, Federal Reserve, Secret Service, and BEP. Based on a comprehensive study by the National Academy of Sciences (NAS) issued in 1993, the Steering Committee then made recommendations for new design and security features to the Secretary of the Treasury, who has statutory authority to approve such changes. More than 120 security features were examined and tested, including those submitted in response to a BEP solicitation, those used in other currencies, and those suggested by the NAS. Evaluation criteria included impact on security, proven reliability, ability to be manufactured in large quantities, and durability over time. Among the features evaluated were holograms, color-shifting films, thread variations, color patterns, and machine-readable enhancements. The strategy of the Design Task Force was to incorporate as many features as could be justified. The security features ultimately selected have proved successful in other countries as well as in test environments at BEP and the Federal Reserve, and since their incorporation into U.S. currency they have been an effective deterrent to counterfeiters.

In its second report, the NAS evaluated features to help those with low vision differentiate between currency denominations. These included variations in size and shape, holes, and other tactile features that the Task Force deemed were not sufficiently durable to be practicable for U.S. currency at this time. The Task Force agreed that a high-contrast feature, such as a large numeral on a light background, would be useful to Americans with low vision. The notes could be easily incorporated into the new series design without compromising the improved security of the new notes or adding cost. A new machine-readable feature was incorporated on the $20 note for the blind that will facilitate development of convenient scanning devices that could identify the note's denomination. The Design Task Force will continue to seek and test new features to make U.S. currency even more secure and more readily usable as technology further evolves.

Recent Studies in Currency Counterfeiting

United States Currency Security Features Counterfeit Deterrence

■ *Counterfeit Deterrent Features for the Next Generation Currency Design,* December 1993, National Research Council, funded by the Department of the Treasury.

Purpose: To analyze and recommend overt counterfeit deterrent feature that could be incorporated into a redesign of U.S. bank notes. Starting with the 1996 series, U.S. paper currency is being redesigned to incorporate anti-counterfeiting features. Features recommended include color-shifting ink, a watermark, microprinting, a security thread, and other features that are difficult to copy.

■ *Advanced Reprographic Systems: Counterfeiting Threat Assessment and Deterrent Measures,* June 1986, National Academy of Sciences, funded by the Bureau of Engraving and Printing.

Purpose: To assess counterfeit threats from specific advanced reprographic equipment and recommend counterfeit deterrents. The study confirmed the counterfeiting threat and recommended action. For the near term, it suggested a combination of conventional deterrent devices, including a security thread.

Features for the Visually Impaired

■ *Currency Features for Visually Impaired People,* 1995, National Research Council, funded by the Bureau of Engraving and Printing.

Purpose: To analyze and recommend overt counterfeit deterrence features that could be incorporated into a redesign of U.S. currency for use by the visually impaired. The study recommended long-range systematic planning as a regular part of the mission within the Department of the Treasury.

Security Features

The Department of the Treasury's Bureau of Engraving and Printing is responsible for producing the new series currency, which, like other U.S. currency, is issued through the Federal Reserve System. The new features found in the Series 1996 $20, $50, and $100 notes include:

- Enlarged off-center portrait
- Watermark
- Fine-line printing patterns
- Color-shifting ink

All the new features were selected after extensive testing and evaluation of approximately 120 bank note security devices, many of which are used successfully by other countries with lower production and circulation demands. Other security features already in use, such as the security thread and microprinting, are included in the new notes and have changed only slightly.

In December 1993, the National Research Council (NRC), funded by the Department of the Treasury, published *Counterfeit Deterrent Features for the Next Generation Currency Design* (see above). This report analyzed and recommended overt counterfeit deterrent features that could be incorporated into a redesign of U.S. bank notes. The developmental costs for the new series were $256,376 to fund the NRC study, and approximately $500,000 to purchase test quantities of features and carry out internal BEP analyses.

Evaluation Criteria

- Effectiveness — Reprographic equipment manufacturers and government scientists tested effectiveness of counterfeit deterrents. They also considered the ease of public and cash handler recognition.
- Durability — Rigorous testing included crumpling, folding, laundering, soiling, and soaking in a variety of solvents, such as gasoline, acids and laundry products.
- Production costs — Research and production expenses will increase the cost of each note by about 2¢. The Federal Reserve System has funded the development and introduction of the new currency through earnings the Federal Reserve receives, primarily from interest on its holdings of U.S. government securities.

Introduction of the Series 1996 Currency

The Series 1996 currency series incorporates new features designed to improve the security of our currency. The Series 1996 $20 note was introduced in the fall of 1998. The new $50 note was introduced in October 1997, and the $100 note was introduced in March 1996. Lower denominations will follow. There will be no recall or devaluation of U.S. currency already in circulation; the United States always honors its currency at full face value, no matter how old.

The issuance of the Series 1996 $20 note has special importance because it is the first redesigned note to be widely used in the United States. It is the most often used of the larger denomination notes and is commonly distributed through automated teller machines (ATMs). All users of U.S. currency should be familiar with the appearance and new security features of these new notes. People who use U.S. currency are the first line of defense against counterfeiting; cash handlers and consumers should examine all notes carefully to guard against counterfeits.

The new Federal Reserve $20 notes will be phased into circulation, replacing older notes as they reach the banking system. This multi-year introduction of the new series is necessary because of the time-intensive printing process and because a sufficient inventory of new notes must be available when the new note is issued to ensure its worldwide availability.

In 1996, the Federal Reserve System and the U.S. Treasury Department began a worldwide public education campaign with two primary objectives:

1. To communicate to the general public there will be no recall or devaluation
2. To provide information that will enable the public, law enforcement personnel, central banks, depository financial institutions, and other cash handlers to authenticate the new series notes

Security Features of the New Design

Appearance

The currency still has a familiar American look. The size of the notes, basic colors, historical figures, and national symbols are not changing. New features were evaluated for their compatibility with the traditional design of U.S. currency.

Watermark

Varying paper density in a small area during the papermaking process forms the watermark. The image is visible as darker and lighter areas when held up to the light. The watermark is a good way to authenticate the note, as it does not copy on color copiers or scanners, thus making it more difficult to use lower denomination paper to print counterfeit notes of higher denominations. The watermark depicts the same historical figure as the engraved portrait.

Color-Shifting Inks

These inks, used in the numeral on the lower right corner of the face of the note, change color when the note is viewed from different angles. The ink appears green when viewed directly and changes to black when the note is tilted.

Fine-Line Printing Patterns

This type of line structure appears normal to the human eye but is difficult for current copying and scanning equipment to resolve properly. The lines are found behind the portrait on the front and around the historic building on the back.

Enlarged Off-Center Portraits

The larger portrait can incorporate more detail, making it easier to recognize and more difficult to counterfeit. It also provides an easy way for the public to distinguish the new design from the old. The portrait is shifted off-center to provide room for a watermark and unique "lanes" for the security thread in each denomination. The slight relocation also reduces wear on most of the portrait by removing it from the center, which is frequently folded. The increased image size can help people with visual impairments identify the note.

Low-Vision Feature

The Series 1996 $20 and $50 notes have a large, dark numeral on a light background on the lower right corner of the back. This numeral, which represents the denomination, helps people with low vision, senior citizens, and others as well because it is easier to read. Also, as mentioned previously, a machine-readable feature has been incorporated for the blind which will facilitate development of convenient scanning devices that, for example, could identify the note as a $20 bill.

Security Thread

A security thread is a thin thread or ribbon running through a bank note substrate. All 1990 series and later notes, except the $1, include this feature. The note's denomination is printed on the thread. Also, the threads of the new $20 and new $50 have graphics in addition to the printed denomination. The denomination number appears in the star field of the flag printed on the thread. The thread in the new notes glows when held under a long-wave ultraviolet light. In the new $20 note, it glows green; in the new $50 note, yellow; in the new $100 note, red. Because it is visible in transmitted light, but not in reflected light, the thread is difficult to copy with a color copier, which uses reflected light to generate an image. Using a unique thread position for each denomination guards against certain counterfeit techniques, such as bleaching ink off a lower denomination and using the paper to "reprint" the bill as a higher value note.

Microprinting

This print appears as a thin line to the naked eye, but the lettering easily can be read using a low-power magnifier. The resolution of most current copiers is not sufficient to copy such fine print. On the newly designed $20 notes, microprinting appears in the lower left corner numeral and along the lower edge ornamentation of the oval framing the portrait. On the $50 notes, microprinting appears on the side borders and in Ulysses Grant's collar. On the $100 note, microprinting appears in the lower left corner numeral and on Benjamin Franklin's coat. In 1990, 1993, and 1995 series notes, "The United States of America" is printed repeatedly in a line outside the portrait frame.

Serial Numbers

Serial numbers on the new currency differ slightly from old currency. The new serial numbers consist of two prefix letters, eight numerals, and a one-letter suffix. The first letter of the prefix designates the series (for example, the letter A will designate 1996). The second letter of the prefix designates the Federal Reserve Bank to which the note was issued. In addition, a universal Federal Reserve seal replaces individual seals for each Reserve Bank.

Notes

The information contained in this chapter is based on research from the U.S. Treasury Department. The information is to their full credit and was provided to the reader as being some of the best government public information available. The U.S. Secret Service, under the supervision of the U.S. Treasury, contributed additional information. Additional publications of interest would include *Currency Facts* (U.S. Department of the Treasury, 1997). Video presentations would include *Know Your Money*, narrated by former U.S. Treasury Secretary Rubin.

Schemes Involving Access Devices

4

When we refer to schemes involving access devices, we refer to criminal acts that are attacks against such devices or processes around the device. These crimes have traditionally been the crime of choice for many because the perpetrators believe that these are victimless crimes. The following categories of schemes are among the most popular.

Credit Cards

The credit card has truly been one of the most innovative technologies of the century. It has increased spending power and helped the world economy. It has also afforded the criminal a means to attack the very system it is intended to protect, our world's economic infrastructure.

The credit card has been attacked or used illegally in many ways since its inception. Clearly, current technology is foiling criminals, due to the diligence mentioned earlier in the text by credit card associations, issuers, and most merchants. They are using technology not only to identify criminals but also to prevent such crimes or attacks from even happening. Credit card issuers such as retail banks, for example, are using early detection systems in the issuing process, as well as in the spending process, to protect their interest and that of their customers.

The process further assures that risks to all concerned can be minimized. The attacks against credit cards are further explained in this chapter according to the various types of attacks. To better understand credit card crimes, you need to understand that the credit card is merely a device. The device, however, is a vehicle that contains a variety of useful information.

Bank Cards

There are several types of bank cards, including check cards and debit cards. These bank cards are defined as being access devices issued by a member financial or like institution to their customers to encourage electronic banking or related transactions, thus allowing such transactions to be available to customers 24 hours a day without the need for person-to-person contact. These cards can be used at point-of-sale terminals, automated teller machines (ATMs), and communications devices, to name a few. Bank cards operate under the same principals as most credit cards.

Check Cards

A check card is tied to an existing bank account or line of credit. The card is used to replace the need to write a draft and automatically transfers the funds to the payee's account electronically. It offers the payee greater assurance of the transaction being approved and paid.

Debit Cards

Debit cards operate much the same way and can be tied to more than one type of account. Debit cards widely used today display the Visa or MasterCard logo which allows customers to use this card as they would a regular Visa or MasterCard credit card. The card transaction simply debits the funds immediately from the customer's account, reducing their balance.

False Applications

A false application is when a person enters false information on a credit application with the intent to receive credit unlawfully and defraud the financial institution. Criminals change information or Social Security numbers, inflate income, or supply other information with the intent to defraud.

Account Takeovers

An account takeover occurs when a person unlawfully causes the takeover of any account by changing information, diverting accounts to their control, or impersonating the lawful account holder or contacts the issuer with such intent causing information to be changed. Generally, when the account is under the criminal's control, it is then used unlawfully for personal or other such illegal gain.

Mail Theft

Mail theft occurs when financial documents or any access devices are mailed via the Postal Service to their lawfully intended customer and they are stolen in the mail stream. In large-scale operations, such stolen mail is generally re-used or sold. Common mail thefts could include a person stealing mail from your mailbox or home. Financial institutions refer to this as a never received issue (NRI). Large-scale operations have targeted mail flow through major airline hubs, stealing mail right out of the aircraft or cargo areas. Postal inspectors in the United States have attempted to control such activity, coordinating airport task forces and working with counterparts in other countries.

Altered Cards

Any access device that is changed in any way to change the appearance or electronic information contained within the device is said to be altered. Criminals often use stolen, valid card numbers on stolen devices to create the appearance of a valid card. This often involves removing the old numbers by heating and ironing the card flat and re-embossing it with the new numbers that are valid. Magnetic stripes on the cards can also be changed electronically with the proper equipment, but chip cards are very difficult to alter and often end up cracked. This generally limits the use of cards to those having only magnetic stripes.

White Plastic

White plastic is the virgin product (plastic card) used to screen or counterfeit an access device. This is also the name given to plastic cards of many colors that are embossed or encoded and can be used as substitutes for fully printed counterfeit cards.

True Counterfeit

A true counterfeit is generally defined as being a counterfeit card using false or stolen information to generate a device for illegal use.

Mail Order/Telephone Fraud/Telemarketing Fraud

Such fraud takes place when a customer is solicited or targeted by an unlawful operation for the sole purpose of selling them a bill of goods. There is no intent to provide the product or services offered, and representations are made to gain profit by means of defrauding the customer or victim. This practice can be accomplished by telephone or via the mail.

Example of Telemarketing Fraud

"Hello, Mrs. Smith, my name is James Monroe from the XYZ Company. You have won a trip to Florida and, for only $49.95 charged to your credit card today for processing fees, we will send you your tickets for an all-expense-paid vacation." (Note that this same scam could be directed to the victim by mail.) The victims comply with such requests and pay for the product, but they never receive the prize. Sometimes they receive their prizes, but it ends up costing them more to upgrade the prize or service. Such a tactic is nothing more than the old come-on! In many cases, after the money is taken from several victims, the company goes out of business, leaving the victim with little or no recourse. Such deception is a common business practice of telemarketing frauds.

Cardholder Fraud

Cardholder fraud occurs when a credit card customer receives a credit card under his own identity but with the intent to defraud the issuer. An example would be if "Lily Chan" applies for and receives a JCB credit card under her own name. She then decides to defraud the issuer by lending the credit card to an accomplice to use on vacation. "Charge it up as you wish," she tells her accomplice, "and when you return, I will attest to being at home and at work and will file an affidavit of fraudulent use with the credit card company." Ms. Chan receives cash money for an agreed percentage spent unlawfully on the card by her counterpart. The credit card company is out the money, and the scheme has netted illegal gain to the team of criminals. This is cardholder fraud.

5 Corrupt Government Employees and Internal Schemes

Case Study #1: Operation Pinch

In 1996, the largest issuer of credit cards in the United States noticed significant losses in several areas of the country. In particular, the New York area was a focal point of the attack. Several other venues were also identified as the scheme unfolded. In the early stages of the investigation, bank investigators, along with their technical counterparts, noticed a trend beginning to emerge almost overnight. The fraud-prevention department of a major bank card issuer noticed questionable point-of-sale transactions at several New York merchants. For the purpose of this case study, all the transactions were fraudulent and being completed at the same area merchants. Preliminary review by bank investigators resulted in a plan to interview all the affected merchants to establish some leads for their law enforcement counterparts. No good leads were established, and the case was at a stalemate. The bank investigators gave their preliminary information to the U.S. Secret Service in New York to try to establish if this case had any similarity to other cases being worked on at the time. Initially, it appeared not to.

The intelligence was also shared with the investigative units of two other banks that were apparently also targeted by the crooks. The investigators from all three banks met in Maryland to review losses and findings and prepared a link analysis to further the investigation. In the meantime, losses were exceeding the millions for the affected banks, but no other financial institutions were complaining of such losses. About 2 weeks into the investigation, high-level sources in the bank wanted answers as to the losses that were mounting. The pressure was building for investigators to solve this case. Databases of cases were reviewed, and one case in particular raised the interest of a bank investigator. In 1992, special agents of the U.S. Secret Service were the lead agents on a case while assigned to the Metro Alien Fraud Task Force in Washington, D.C. A search warrant was executed in a fraud scheme, and the search netted a major plot by suspects to steal and sell information from the Social Security Administration. A document was uncovered in the search which was later identified as a Social Security numident. This is a 4×5 dot matrix computer printout showing a person's Social Security identifiers; most importantly, it included the claimant's mother's maiden name.

After reviewing this earlier investigation, the bank investigator contacted Special Agents of the Social Security Administration's Office of the Inspector General. The bank investigator asked his counterparts at the Social Security Administration to run about 30 of the account holders' names and Social Security numbers through the Social Security system to see if there were any hits on them by insiders. Agents of the Social Security Administration thought initially that the idea was improbable; however, they eventually were convinced by the earlier case information from the Secret Service that it was a possibility.

A link analysis of the cards in question indicated compromises of the mothers' maiden names (I believe Sherlock Homes said something like "you need to discount the improbable to understand what is probable"). The mother's maiden name is often used as a method of authentication, as a PIN identifier. It was the only good lead. Social Security Administration agents were contacted at about 12 noon on a Friday with this information. At 4:30 p.m., the bank investigator was informed that one employee of the Social Security Administration ("Ms. A") in New York had accessed at least 90% of the files provided for analysis, and for no apparent reason. The infamous electronic fingerprint, her computer access code, identified this suspect. A Social Security Administration agent and the bank investigator were immediately instructed by their superiors to fly to New York to brief their New York law enforcement counterparts at the Social Security Administration, the Secret Service, and the Postal Inspection Service. The decision was made by the Inspector General in Charge for the Social Security Administration in New York that this employee should be interviewed as a suspect. The suspect eventually told the entire story. Case intelligence revealed that her supervisor approached her to help another city agency with case intelligence and background information. This conspirator was a West African male working as a Welfare Investigator who had convinced the Social Security supervisor that he was on official business and needed information. Ms. A was assigned to assist him. This Welfare Investigator, of course, did not have the best interests of his clients in mind. He had plotted to use his position to unlawfully obtain data.

For purposes of obtaining illegal credits cards, his relationship with Ms. A grew; she was cut in on the scheme and was compensated for providing unknown amounts of data. This enterprise became a supply-and-demand business within the Social Security Administration. The business evolved to the point where several other Social Security offices became involved in the scheme, and over 10,000 Social Security case files were comprised. This matter was now classified as a major organized crime ring that had infiltrated the Social Security Administration.

A bank investigator uncovered another break from the Florida field office. He and a postal inspector had what they thought to be an unrelated case out of New Orleans and Atlanta, but another part of the West African organized crime cell was uncovered. This case involved theft of mail from airports and post offices, in addition to the stealing of data from the Social Security Administration. To date, over 30 "insiders" working with external accomplices have been arrested and convicted of this major crime. This is a textbook example of corrupt government officials entrusted by the taxpayers to serve and protect their most valuable personal information. If you were the investigator, on this case, how would you investigate this type of case?

Questions To Ask

1. What components should you be looking for to get started? Consider prioritizing the case: Who is the victim? What impact will the situation have on the case? What do the initial facts or criminal complaints suggest happened here?
2. Are you the law enforcement agency who is going to work the case (i.e., federal prosecutor, states attorney, district attorney)? Review the potential violations of law and determine where venue best exists.
3. If you are a financial crimes investigator in the private sector, what agency is going to work with you on this referral? Alternatively, is this just another internal case for which the company will take corrective action? Review your fiduciary responsibilities carefully at this point, should this be the case. Many venues would seriously consider prosecuting for concealment of certain crimes.

At this point, you should be ready to push away from your desk. Many financial types of cases require "pounding the pavement" for facts, interviews, and gathering evidence to result in successful resolution of your case. A key concern to keep in mind in regard to internal cases is that they never turn out pretty! Someone is going to be offended by the investigation and the fact that the crime actually took place on their watch. Move methodically and do not let pressure from above interfere with your good investigative techniques. Private-sector cases are particularly vulnerable to lawsuits, so go by the book and document everything. Keep good case notes and have reputable witnesses during any internal interview or interrogation.

Case Study Review and Assignment

Review the following questions and answer them as if you were assigned to or working the case.

1. What investigative leads were evident that stimulated bank investigators to task their resources at Social Security and the Office of the Inspector General?

2. What is the importance of creating a database of such information for research purposes?
3. What is your understanding of the criminal violations of law? Explain.
4. What would be your plan for the investigation if you had been the law enforcement agency?

Suppose you received this case as a referral from the bank investigators, and also suppose that you did not have prior intelligence of the 1992 Secret Service case:

5. Why was the U.S. Postal Inspection Service involved in this case?
6. Why was the U.S. Secret Service involved in this case?
7. What questions, as an investigator, would you have had during the preliminary stages?
8. Who were the merchants where the fraud took place?
9. How and when would you disseminate information about your case to other law enforcement or investigative groups (i.e., banks, retailers, etc.)?
10. What would be the role of prosecutors in this case?
11. How would you prioritize such a major case with your large case load?

Merchant Collusion

Sometimes a merchant will work in concert with the criminal to perpetrate the fraud. Not only do employees working for merchants get involved in these schemes, but the company owners do, as well, and it happens in greater numbers than you would think. The schemes can vary from simply stealing information from legitimate customers to illegally processing credit card transactions for non-approved venders.

Case Study #2: Operation Take You for a Ride

In 1992, a New York City car service driver got the idea that he could really take his customers for a ride. Not only would he provide them with limousine service to their business destinations, but he would also steal their credit card information after processing the fare. He would make two copies of the credit card using a portable embosser and file one with his company for payment on the day of the fare. He would take the second copy to his brother's electronics shop and put through a bogus transaction using the signed credit card voucher. It appeared, then, that the cardholder not only took a ride in the limousine, but later he also went shopping and brought a $50 camera or similar product.

The owner of the electronics shop would get paid and split the profits with his brother. This scheme continued for months until it was discovered and the suspects arrested. The shop had already closed, however, and all the money was gone. The suspects made several thousand dollars in charges and further defrauded the victims by asking for their driver's licenses for identification, information they then used to further their fraudulent schemes — accounts were established, credit abused, etc.

Questions

1. How could the investigator in this case conduct a link analysis to identify the suspects?
2. What would your resources be?
3. What evidence would you need to gather?
4. What safeguards can you suggest to prevent such a crime from occurring?
5. How would you get information about all the victims?

Investigation of Financial Access Devices

6

Conducting a financial crime investigation involving access devices is different from most investigations. It can be very difficult, with little or no training, to understand the mechanics of the crime, let alone the scientific or technical aspects. You simply cannot fake your way through such an investigation. You need to have a good understanding of how the crime could have been committed. Now, we might discover that Bob stole a credit card from his girlfriend and used it illegally to purchase car parts for $600. Do we understand, though, how to track the credit information and what resources and documentation are required? Richard Stine of the Frederick County States Attorney Office in Maryland is a veteran law enforcement investigator, with over 25 years of experience. In his words, "When I first started investigating, much of what I did was investigative intuition — you most likely knew who your perpetuators were. Today it is a whole new ballgame. The criminals are high tech in these types of crimes and in most cases just a little smarter. Or so they think. What I need to get across to police officers and investigators is that in these types of investigations, you need to stay up on the technology."

How Do I Start My Investigation?

Let us create a scenario: Monday morning, you receive a report from a person (we will call her Mary) who states that her credit card company called her questioning several large overseas purchases. Mary, however, did not make the purchases. The last time she used her card was when she stopped to buy gas at a point-of-sale pump on

Saturday night after going to dinner at the China Kitchen Restaurant with her college roommate (Kathy). Mary had paid the $34 bill for the meal with her credit card. After leaving the gas station, the two women went to a club for an hour and paid cash for their two drinks. They both went home after that and spent Sunday studying for exams. They made no further purchases and had the credit card at all times. What happened and how would you start your investigation?

1. What aspects of this case are unusual?
2. The complainant had her credit card at the time of the report, so how could it have been used illegally?
3. Who is suspected here?
4. What facts in this investigation require technical knowledge of financial crimes?

What Facts Do I Need To Start?

Before you continue your investigation, you need to understand what information you need to gather, which is where your training and experience come into play. First, remain open and objective. Do not try to solve the case quickly, as you most likely will not be successful. Review the facts, and come up with a written investigative plan — avoid improvising as your investigation moves along. The following is a suggested plan for the case presented above.

1. In regard to your complainants, what is their background, criminal history, etc.? Review prior case reports, if any, made by the alleged victims.
2. What details are important in the case?
3. Review all the facts that were initially presented to the person taking the report (if that was not you), and interview the victims in depth. When more than one victim is involved, conduct the interviews separately.
4. In many cases of financial crimes, time is not always on your side. Often in credit card cases, the victims will not find out about the crimes until after they receive their monthly statements from the credit card company. Hence, little time can be wasted recovering evidence and developing further leads.
5. Decide who you can interview next, after the victims, and who your resources might be. In this case, what about the credit cards investigators? They can often be essential to your investigation

Documents you will need from the credit card companies include:

1. Account statements to show account history and locations of most charges.
2. Authorization logs and charge media to show the actual dates of the transactions, times when the sales were authorized, and the media used (charge slips or drafts), all of which will be evidence necessary for further forensic evaluation.

3. Obtain sufficient handwriting samples from your complainant. This will help identify any documents that the forensics examiner, or you, reviews. In some cases, you will find that the suspect identified during the investigation is your complainant.
4. The credit card investigators can assist you with obtaining videotapes of the transactions (if available) from the merchants involved. Act quickly, as tapes are often recycled after a few days. During extensive interviews with these merchants, you will want to obtain any credit card media they might have retained and the names of employees who completed the transactions in question.
5. Ask for any affidavits of fraud filed by customers of these merchants.

Facts and Questions for the Investigator

Facts:

1. Your victims are telling the truth.
2. No merchants or staff are involved.
3. The credit card is accounted for at all times.

Questions:

1. How did the card get used illegally?
2. How did it get used overseas?
3. How did the credit card company know to call the customer?
4. What do you do next?

How Did It Happen?

The facts of this case are quite simple … if you understand the technical issues about credit cards and transactions. The victim, Mary, was telling the truth and was victimized; however, it was due to some carelessness on her behalf. When she and her roommate stopped at the gas station and used the card to pump gas, they used a point-of-sale terminal, which allows customers to put their credit cards in the machine and, if credit is available, to buy gas. Mary did this and received her gas. What she failed to do was take her receipt out of the pump when she was done.

Some gas stations still show the credit card number on the receipt as well as a name. Unfortunately, someone was staking out this particular gas station, looking for receipts left behind. He simply pumped a few dollars' worth of gas and took the receipt without raising any suspicion. He was part of a ring and sold Mary's credit card number, as well as several others he had taken that week, to a New Jersey counterpart. This individual then sold them again to a colleague in the United

Kingdom. Hence, the numbers were used to make illegal purchases in England less than 24 hours after they were stolen. If you did not understand the technology, do you think you would have been able to solve this case? What would you do to further this investigation with your foreign counterparts?

Available Resources

Available resources for such investigations include the U.S. Secret Service, Interpol, and New Scotland Yard in England. Coordinate your efforts with the credit card investigators, as they always have foreign offices that can assist you.

Integrated Circuit Cards

7

What Are They?

Integrated circuit card (ICC), also known as Chip Cards, Smart Cards, and Memory Cards, refer to a standard plastic card with an embedded integrated circuit. Such cards are used for a variety of applications, such as telephone cards, identification, access control, mass transit, and financial transactions. The vast majority of ICCs in use are telephone cards, which are relatively simple devices having limited functionality and security. Financial transaction cards differ from other cards in that they utilize secure microprocessors that support greater functionality and a high level of security. They are further defined by industry- and issuer-specific standards.

Microprocessor-based ICCs used as financial transaction cards can be thought of as a personal computer within a card, although obviously there are major differences in memory and input/output functionality. All memory in the card is located on the integrated circuit (chip); there is no disk drive or other auxiliary memory. All communication is by means of the contacts on the surface of the card. These contacts are essentially a serial communications channel, which is always under the control of the operating system and security parameters. There are no other input/output devices such as keyboards, displays, printers, etc.

There are typically three kinds of memory on the card: read-only memory (ROM), electrically erasable programmable read-only memory (EEPROM), and random access memory (RAM). The operating system and application programs are stored in ROM and EEPROM. Cardholder-specific data and transaction data are stored in EEPROM. RAM is used for temporary storage during the execution of applications.

Memory is also segmented into security levels having various access attributes. As examples, some data (public) can be read by anyone but can only be altered under password control. Other data (private) can be under password control for both reading and alteration. Finally, some data (secret) can never be read externally but can be altered under password control. Cryptography is a key aspect of card security. All financial cards can execute a symmetrical encryption algorithm, currently DES (digital encryption standard). The newest cards can also execute an asymmetrical encryption algorithm, currently RSA (Rivest, Shamir, Adleman; named for the inventors of the public key system). Critical data, such as encryption keys, are unique for each card. In addition to the software security, there are numerous hardware security features that make examination or alteration of the card logic or data extremely difficult. In combination, these hardware and software security measures create a secure device. The cost to compromise the card security should exceed any potential economic gain.

How Are They Used?

The activities of any transaction can be grouped into four processes:

1. Authentication of the parties (are they who they say they are, and what privileges do they have?)
2. Authorization of the transaction (do the parties have the resources necessary and are they authorized to expend these resources?)
3. Execution of the transaction
4. Documentation of the transaction

A secure ICC can increase the security and accuracy of each of these processes.

Authentication

Because the card can securely store unique information, such as encryption keys, a cryptographic exchange between the card and terminal is used to ensure the authenticity of both parties. The specifics of this exchange will vary with the algorithms and key management policies being used. Authentication of the cardholder can be accomplished by comparing a PIN or biometrics information supplied by the cardholder with data stored within the card. Thus, with a high level of certainty, the terminal determines that the card is authentic; at the same time, the card detects that the terminal is authentic, and the cardholder is revealed as being the *true* cardholder. In addition, this authentication process can be accomplished in an "off-line" mode (i.e., the card issuer does not have to be contacted at the time of the transaction). Such authentication is important for face-to-face transactions and will be even more important for the growing number of electronic commerce transactions.

Authorization

Each card can store cardholder-specific risk management parameters. Such parameters might include limits regarding the number and/or value of transactions permitted without going to the issuer for authorization. Also, it is possible to temporarily disable (block) a card. Using another cryptographic exchange, the issuer can instruct the card to refuse further transactions until the correct "unblock" command is used. Thus, a stolen card can be prevented from executing additional transactions in ICC mode.

Execution

Once authentication and authorization are accomplished, the transaction can be executed.

Documentation

The card can provide a digital signature (certificate) of the transaction for the merchant. Information about the card, the merchant, and the transaction is combined and cryptographically "signed" with a key unique to the card. This certificate can provide strong defense against disputed transactions. Like a personal computer, microprocessor cards can execute applications. The French banks initiated the first major ICC implementation of supporting debit transactions. Using the security features of the card, off-line debit transactions could be conducted, which decreased communication costs and virtually eliminated counterfeit transactions of French cards within France.

Electronic purse applications have been implemented in a number of locations around the world. A specific amount of value is securely transferred (loaded) to the card. This amount is then reduced as the card is used. Some cards, such as telephone cards, can be loaded only once, while others can be reloaded. Most financial ICCs currently support one of these applications. Some cards currently being issued will, or are expected to, support combinations of the above plus non-financial applications such as affinity, rewards, specialty purse functions (company/school cafeteria, parking, toll), or mass transit functions.

Implications for the Investigator

Directly attacking the ICC technology will be difficult; therefore, criminals will seek other approaches. Initially, they may look for locations that do not have ICC-compatible terminals. More sophisticated criminals may attempt to create counterfeit cards. To do so, however, they will need the data used by the cryptographic processes, the key. The end effect will be an increased emphasis on theft of data rather than cards. Investigators will need to know where and how these data are stored, who has access to the data, and the audit trails employed. Investigators will need a better understanding of the payment system and at least a fundamental understanding of encryption and key management processes.

Figure 1

Encryption

Encryption is the process of changing intelligible data (clear text) into unintelligible data (cipher text) and, with the correct information, back into intelligible data (see Figure 1). This process is accomplished using mathematical algorithms and "keys" — long strings of binary (one or zero) bits. The algorithms used are typically well known, just as the general design of a physical lock is well understood. The uniqueness (secrecy) of the data is achieved through the uniqueness of the key. Just as a physical lock can be keyed to a specific pattern of notches, an algorithm can be keyed to a specific series of bits.

The strength of a lock is based upon its design and the number of possible key combinations. The same is true of an encryption algorithm. It is impractical to "pick" a well-designed algorithm. Instead, attacks are based upon determining which key was used. Long keys, which offer more combinations, are important. For example, a 56-bit DES key has approximately 74,000,000,000,000,000 possible combinations. Even more important, is protection of the keys. This discipline is referred to as "key management".

There are two kinds of encryption algorithms. Each has advantages and disadvantages. Symmetrical algorithms use the same key for encryption and decryption, hence the name. Asymmetrical algorithms use a pair of keys. One is called the private key; the other, the public key. These keys are different but mathematically related. Although they are related, it is not feasible to infer one from the other.

Symmetrical algorithms are fast, up to 1000 times faster than asymmetrical algorithms. Symmetrical algorithms typically have shorter keys, 56 to 160 bits, compared to 512- to 2048-bit asymmetrical keys. While symmetrical algorithms are fast, they do have disadvantages in the area of key management. For secrecy, each pair of users needs to have a unique key. When the number of users becomes large, management of these keys can become a significant task. Another drawback is the need for key security at all locations. This is an issue when one user is a low-cost remote device.

Asymmetrical algorithms are typically slow; however, they allow for a number of key management opportunities. Because the keys are different, it is not necessary to secure a public key. A user can freely distribute the public key, even placing it in a public directory. Anyone can use this key to encrypt a message to the user, but only the user can decrypt the message using the private key. Variations of this attribute facilitate establishment of temporary symmetrical keys between strangers so secure communications can be accomplished. Other variations provide data integrity and allow for convenient user and data authentication. Asymmetrical algorithms are very

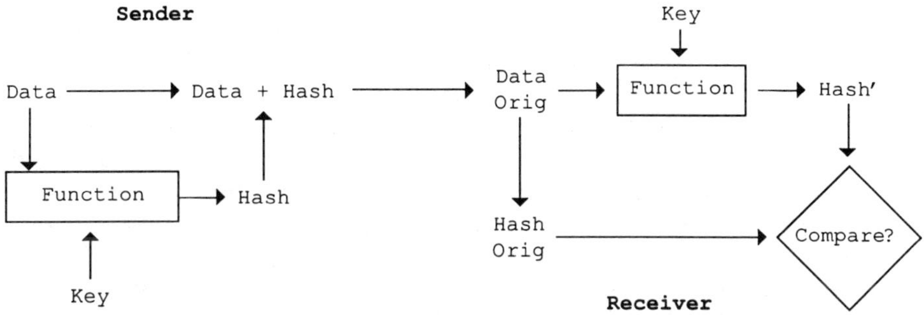

Figure 2

useful for authentication and for exchanging temporary symmetrical keys between parties, even total strangers, as long as they mutually trust a third party. In practice, the two forms of encryption are used in combination.

How Is Encryption Used?

Encryption offers three essential capabilities: privacy, data integrity, and authentication. Common examples of privacy include transmission of personal identification numbers (PINs) or other sensitive data. The process is as depicted above in Figure 1. Data integrity has long been used in wholesale banking to ensure the integrity of messages. Using symmetrical encryption, the process is straightforward (see Figure 2).

There are many variations to this process. The basics remain the same. Data, or selected elements of the data, are input to a mathematical function. Frequently, but not always, this is a cryptographic function. The output of the function, which is considerably shorter than the input data, is appended to the message and is referred to by many names — hash, MAC, message digest, etc. The recipient of the message separates the appended hash data from the message and replicates the process, using the same key if the process is cryptographic. The two hashes, Hash and Hash′, are then compared.

Assuming the hashes match, the recipient can be certain that the massage has not been altered. Note, unless the key used is shared only between the sender and receiver, the recipient cannot be sure who originated the message (authentication). Also, the message could be a duplicate of an earlier message, a "playback attack". To prevent playback attacks, a sequence number and/or time-date stamp are added to the message.

Authentication, using symmetrical encryption, is based upon the assumption that keys are kept secret between the two participants. A common method used for authentication is the encryption of a random number. The sender arbitrarily selects a random number and encrypts it. The random number is sent to the recipient, who encrypts the number with the shared secret key and sends the result back to the sender. The sender compares the two results. If the results match, it is presumed the two parties can trust each other. This technique is often used by ICCs and the device with which they are communicating. The technique is used sparingly, as it is subject to certain attacks.

Asymmetrical encryption offers a number of new authentication possibilities. Fundamental to these processes is the assumption that private keys are not shared with anyone. Only the owner of the private key knows its value. In practice, the owner normally does not know it. Only his crytographic processor "knows" it. Public keys are freely distributed, and the recipients are sure to whom the public key belongs.

Authentication (am I sure who created these data?), integrity (am I sure the data have not been modified?), and privacy are obtained with processes that are similar to symmetrical encryption processes but utilize the unique attributes of asymmetrical encryption. In general, processes similar to the following are used.

For authentication, a digital signature of the message is created using the sender's private key and is appended to the message. To save space, this signature is often the encrypted version of a hash or digest of the message. The recipient repeats the hashing process, decrypts the signature using the sender's public key, and compares. If the two match, the recipient can be sure that the message originated from the sender as long as the recipient is sure that the public key being used truly belongs to the sender. Message integrity is achieved as a by-product of the above process. If the signatures did not match, either the data had been modified or someone else sent the message. For privacy, the message is encrypted and sent. The recipient uses the sender's public key to decrypt the message.

Impact to the Investigator

Historical forms of authentication rely upon card attributes, which are supposed to be inspected at the point of sale. Such inspection can be questionable, however. Also, with high-quality counterfeiting devices readily available, it is increasingly difficult for even motivated lay people to identify counterfeits. Therefore, the industry is turning to encryption. Is the card authentic? Are the data being presented authentic? Is the reading device authentic? Is the person presenting the card the true cardholder?

It is unlikely that criminals will attempt to attack the encryption algorithms themselves. Instead, they will attack weak implementations of cryptographic processes. If a compromise occurs, investigators will need to understand how encryption processes work, at least at a fundamental level.

Biometrics

What Is Biometrics?

Biometrics is the measurement (metric) of a physical attribute (bio) of an individual. It is, in effect, a measurement of who we are. Biodynamics, the measurement of a physical activity (what we do), is often included with biometrics. Humans perform a form of biometrics every time we recognize someone's face, either in person or with a representative image, a picture. Unfortunately, humans are not always present at a transaction, and even when they are they are notoriously unreliable. Computers have the potential to be more reliable and more accurate.

How Does Biometrics Work?

Human bodies are amazingly unique, and a wide variety of means have been devised to measure and quantify allegedly unique attributes. Using such attributes, it is possible to search for a match against other attributes stored in databases (e.g., using AFIS, an automated fingerprint identification system). Alternatively, one can match the measured attributes of an individual to those previously measured and stored. This latter process is often referred to as one-to-one authentication.

For financial transactions, it is only necessary to determine that the person presenting the card is, with a high level of assurance, the true cardholder. The comparison template would be recorded on the magnetic stripe, or more likely within the integrated circuit. Authentication is a simpler process than searching a database. As a result, a number of methods are possible. However, due to a number of factors such as cost, size, and reliability of measuring devices and personal intrusiveness, only a small number of methods have broad acceptance:

- Fingerprints
- Hand geometry
- Facial recognition
- Iris pattern recognition
- Voice recognition
- Finger geometry
- Retinal pattern recognition

Each method has advantages and disadvantages. Proper selection is based upon a trade off of factors, such as:

- User acceptance — How intrusive is the reading process? Is there a social stigma associated with it?
- Human factors — Is the reading device user friendly? Can users interface with it easily?
- Accuracy — How accurate is the process in theory? How accurate is the process when user and environmental factors are considered?
- Reliability — Will the system provide repeatable results?
- Speed — How long does it take to read, process, and compare the information that has been read?
- Template size — How much storage is required to provide a unique measurement?
- Cost — How much does the system cost, including reader, comparison means, and data storage?

Implications for the Investigator

Personal identification numbers are currently used for cardholder authentication. PINs are a form of password and, like passwords, can be compromised. They can be extorted. Biometrics offers a superior method of cardholder authentication. With an ideal biometrics system, the problem of lost, stolen, or non-received cards and account take-over would be eliminated. Counterfeits would be drastically reduced because the criminal would have to be able to provide identifying information.

Currently, broad usage of biometrics authentication for financial transactions is not practical. Cost, storage requirements, accuracy, and reliability are all issues. Once these issues are resolved, there is still the question of user acceptance; however, the trends indicate that these issues will be resolved one day. Implementation of ICCs will resolve many of the issues. Also, biometrics authentication is being used increasingly for other applications, such as access control and government entitlement programs. With this increased usage, greater user acceptance may result. Of course, when implemented, biometrics authentication systems will not be perfect. Even though it may not be easy, most systems can be compromised. When biometric systems are implemented, the investigator will need to understand the limitations of the process.

Organized Crime Enterprises

8

When we hear the term "organized crime", we generally picture the organizations involved as they have been depicted on television or the silver screen. Such groups are very real, however, and have a tremendous effect on financial and related type crimes.

What Is Organized Crime?

INTERPOL describes organized crime as:[1]

> *Any enterprise or group of persons engaged in a continuing illegal activity which has, as its primary purpose, the generation of profits regardless of national boundaries.*

The United Nations' Economic and Social Council adopted this definition of organized crime:[2]

1. Organized crime is a confederation of criminal individuals or groups that come together because of economic needs, closely resembling the feudal bands which existed in mediaeval Europe before the nation-state emerged. Economic gain is achieved by supplying illegal goods and services in an illegal manner.
2. It involves conspiratorial criminal activity, usually involving the hierarchical coordination of a number of persons in planning and execution of illegal acts, or in the pursuit of legitimate objectives by illegal means. It involves a permanent

commitments at least by key members. In terms of hierarchical coordination, members must be part of a set structure with well-defined roles.

3. Organized crime groups have a tendency to establish a monopoly or near monopoly in providing illegal goods and services to customers, since higher profits are guaranteed in this manner.
4. Organized crime does not limit itself to patently illicit undertakings or illegal services. It also includes such sophisticated activities as money laundering through legitimate business and computer manipulation. It infiltrates many kinds of profitable, legal endeavors.
5. Organized crime uses predatory tactics, such as intimidation, violence, and corruption. These tactics may be sophisticated and subtle or crude, overt, and direct. They are used to secure economic gain through a monopoly in illegal goods and services, as well as to infiltrate legitimate enterprises and to corrupt public officials.

This chapter will provide an overview of some organized crime groups to give the reader a basic understanding of them and to identify some clear differences. We need to recognize that all cultural groups have members that break the law; however, we need to avoid labeling an entire group as criminals simply because of its cultural background. We live in a world that has become a cultural melting pot; it is what makes the world the diverse place that it is. As investigators, our job is to understand these cultural differences and plan our investigations accordingly.

We will now discuss some of the most prevalent groups in operation today. Culture and years of individual sociological traits and criminal activity have clearly identified certain sectors as organized groups. Criminologists and other similar professionals have studied these groups in great depth to find a common trait, which can generally be traced back to their culture or roots. The concept of culture, going back even to the first humans, involves rules of conduct and how we deal with each other — where we live, what we eat, and how we dress, as well as language and the unspoken word. There are also territorial, religious, and other sociological issues that affect particular cultures, as well.

Many of these organized crime groups have migrated to all parts of the world. They have claimed territories and bought businesses and real estate with illegal moneys, and their movement has threatened many sectors of legitimate business and real estate. What is the real impact of organized crime in a country? One study concluded that the impact was nearly $40 billion a year in Canada alone. The yearly direct cost of these crimes was $17 billion. The study further concluded that pain and suffering, when considered, more than doubled the annual cost. It was also noted in the study that one in four Canadians was a victim of a criminal act.[3]

Examples of Some Traditional Organized Crime Groups

The Italian Mafia (La Cosa Nostra), Russian Gangsterism, Asian Triads, and the Nigerian (West African) Crime Group are cells of criminal entities within their respective cultures. As indicated earlier, not all members of these particular cultures are criminals; we are addressing very specific cells within each of these cultures.

The Italian Mafia

These are the guys that the movies portray as lovers of great food and wine. They are religious and very family oriented. You know the ones we mean. The plot of the story usually involves turf wars or territorial rights and a godfather who orders hits on another family. Talk about stereotypes!

The Mafia originated in Sicily in the 19th century when Arab forces occupied the area. Members of the group fled to the nearby mountains to seek refuge and formed a secret society they called the Mafia (the Arabic word for refuge). Initially, the society's intentions were honorable — to promote a sense of family. It was not until the early 1900s that organized crime became associated with the Mafia. Members of the Mafia who saw America as the land of opportunity arrived and cornered the market on alcohol during Prohibition. This is when the leaders began to be elected and territories created. These very organized cells of crime families often controlled politics and commerce in one form or another. Some of the initial enterprises these families controlled included:

- Prohibition (alcohol)
- Gambling
- Counterfeiting
- Prostitution
- Money laundering
- Tobacco
- Drugs

The Mafia is very much associated with illegal market enterprises. These are typically enterprises that arrange contract types of agreements among the participants. The only catch is that these contracts are enforceable only by their rules, not those of a court of competent jurisdiction. It is an organized business scheme structured to enforce rules, to profit, and to punish violators. The success of a particular business structure is generally related to the size of the territory controlled. All members of a particular Mafia business structure receive some sort of protection from the Mafia, sort of a member benefit. Other characteristic activities of the Mafia include their influence in the law enforcement community and the judiciary. When a Mafia group controls a venue, it is serious business for all the players. Control such as this is a major threat to lawful economic growth. The Mafia monopolies in local communities discourage new business and control and even drive out old investors and similar business enterprises.

In the 1970s and early 1980s, the areas of southern Italy with the highest growth rates were found to be those having the lowest levels of both organized and conventional crime; whereas, those areas with the greatest Mafia presence were the only economically stagnant regions of Italy. In a study (survey) of young Italian industrialists, almost 27% of the respondents in the three regions of Italy where organized crime is the most established claimed to have decided not to invest in their area because of criminal pressure. In the same three regions, 58% claimed that they had withdrawn tenders for public contracts as a consequence of criminal threats or political pressure.

Russian Organized Crime

The migration of Russian organized crime cells to many parts of the world has been cause for great concern. In 1994, the Russian Ministry of Internal Affairs reported that 25% of the gross national income of Russia was derived from organized crime activity. Nearly 6000 crime cells or groups have been identified. Their primary involvement includes:

- Money laundering
- Drugs
- Extortion
- Fraud schemes

Russian President Yeltsin issued a decree entitled "On the Urgent Measures To Defend the Population Against Gangsterism and Other Kinds of Organized Crime" on June 14, 1994. The law suspended many existing laws that protected individual rights. Needless to say, it was very controversial, but it was supported by most Russians. This measure was enacted to help control economic criminalization attributed to organized crime and to encourage development of legitimate businesses. President Yeltsin also hoped that his decree would be the turning point in the fight against organized crime. The United States supported this decree; FBI director Louis Freeh made a statement that, "Organized crime in Russia threatens not only the safety of this country but the safety of the United States. To date the unfortunate part of this massive effort is that due to the social and economic deterioration of Russia's infrastructures, the Decree has not yielded the anticipated results."

In 1997, President Yeltsin admitted that the criminal world had openly challenged the state and had launched into an open competition with it; he warned that there was corruption at every level of power. There was concern at the time about the threat by Russian organized crime groups against U.S. national security and law enforcement interests.[4]

Asian Gangs/Triads[5]

Asian organized crime, as many can attest, has been on the rise in the past few years. These particular groups are very difficult to deal with and truly require a particular level of expertise. There are so many rules or cultural codes to follow that typical investigators simply cannot bluff their way through investigations of these groups. The rules of interview and interrogation are very different and need to be followed to net good results.

In general, the Asian organized crime groups have been very attracted to financial crimes. Their claim to fame has been in the area of counterfeit money and credit cards. The most well-known triads come out of Hong Kong. This term "triad" is more commonly used by the British; in reality, the correct term is *Hung Mun* (secret society or dark society). Understanding the true culture and proper use of the language is key to establishing credibility within these communities. The investigator must make an effort to understand the subtleties of the culture and appreciate the history of criminal activities with which the Asian community has been dealing for centuries. These secret societies have been in existence for over 300 years. They are a result of the unrest between two dynasties trying to gain control over China.

Nigerian (West African) Crime Groups

For the last 10 years or so, the criminals associated with West African crime cells (or, specifically, tribal groups such as the Ebu'os) have found it very profitable to enter into the financial crimes arena. They leave a trail of fraud schemes and related crimes from the time they leave Nigeria to their arrival in the United Kingdom or United States.

Nigeria is a country of little or no recordkeeping; very few records, such as birth certificates, marriage documents, and driver's permits, exist. This lack of records has resulted in the opportunity for persons to assume identities, travel away from their homeland, and cause great havoc for law enforcement personnel who try to identify and track them. Even when they are identified and deported back, they seem to reappear under new identities to continue in their criminal enterprises, such as their significant drug-trafficking operations, particularly the distribution of heroin.

How has this group been so successful at getting into other countries, remaining there, and enhancing their criminal activity? One advantage they have has already been identified — the lack of proper records and documentation. It is relatively simple for them to use deceptive and illegal methods to leave their country, never intending to return. They have been able to secure temporary visas or passports indicating intentions ranging from being a tourist to being a visiting student. They then abuse the system and simply overstay their passport and visa rights. By this time, they have hooked up with their native counterparts and have only one thing in mind — to support their new lifestyle away from the poverty of Nigeria by committing fraud and an array of financial and drug-related crimes.

A favorite technique of many of them is for the men to seek the confidence of women and to promise them the world and to return them to Nigeria as members of their (bogus) royal families or tribal groups. As seen in our earlier Social Security case, they use the women to help perpetrate their crimes. This is a move in a new direction by this group; in the earlier stages of their criminal activity, they could be identified rather readily because of the tribal scars on their faces or characteristic handwriting used on fraudulent documents (ranging from credit cards to employment applications). Black, non-Nigerian women have become significant pawns today, offering cover for males who play the role of puppeteer by directing and pulling strings to force them to act on their behalf and to avoid detection.

One of the most significant crimes attributed almost entirely to Nigerians is Advance Fee Fraud (4-1-9 Fraud), which is named after the Nigerian law that identifies such fraud crimes. The scam involves targeting an individual or company and sending a letter or fax that has all the appearance of coming from a foreign government official. These letters are very convincing. The offer typically advises that large sums of money need to be transferred into the recipient's bank account. The recipients are chosen due to their stature in the business world and because they can be trusted; however, the recipients are expected to travel to Nigeria. It is also requested that bank account numbers and other important information (i.e., letterhead, company seals, etc.) be provided. Other aspects of the scam include currency transfers and conversions to acceptance by cash on delivery of an array of goods and services. The proposed benefit to the person or company receiving the letter from Nigeria is the promise to pay commissions for handling the transactions.

In June of 1995, an American actually traveled to Nigeria only to be confronted with threats and harassment to force compliance. This person was found murdered in Lagos, Nigeria. This case was extreme, no doubt, but many persons from around the globe have fallen victim to these scams and have traveled to Nigeria, only to be greeted by impostors claiming to be public officials, ambassadors, or heads of government who need to complete the deals. They greet their victims at the airport, but then hold out their hands out for bribes to escort the victims to their phony leaders.

Law enforcement agencies around the world have targeted these crimes as a global problem and have joined forces to try to establish credible relationships with Nigerian officials. In the Appendix, we have included a bill proposed in the United States to help combat and enforce 4-1-9 crimes. Many venues have presented and approved similar laws.

Notes

1. The Interpol definition was adopted by the General Assembly in 1998 by member countries.
2. *Report of the Secretary General,* Commission on Crime Prevention and Criminal Justice, United Nations' Economic and Social Council, Second Session, Vienna, 1993.
3. Study conducted by the Fraser Institute, Burnaby, British Columbia, 1993.
4. From President Boris Yeltsin's 1997 State of the State Address.
5. Recommended reading: Daye, Douglas D., *A Law Enforcement Sourcebook of Asian Crime and Cultures, Tactics, and Mindsets,* CRC Press, Boca Raton, FL, 1997.

Investigative Resources Available from Industry

9

The financial crime investigative community offers an array of technical, investigative, and monetary support for major investigations. In particular, the International Association of Financial Crimes Investigators (IAFCI), which represents over 4000 industry and law enforcement entities throughout the world, is the most recognized source of support and information. With its members represented globally, the organization is best known for it pro-active approach to reducing fraud and related crimes. This organization has membership ranging from the U.S. Secret Service and Postal Inspection Service to the Royal Canadian Mounted Police and New Scotland Yard. The industries represented include such companies as Visa, MasterCard International, American Express, JCB, Barclays Bank, and hundreds of other foreign and domestic retailers and financial institutions. The IAFCI can be contacted on the Web at IAFCI.org.

In the private sector, consulting firms such as Catoctin Consultants, in Maryland, offer the government and private sector an excellent international resource group under one roof. They can be contacted on the Web at catoctinconsultants.com.

Forensics

10

Introduction

The purpose of this chapter on forensics is to familiarize the reader with how investigators and the forensic scientist can, and should, work together in the search for truth. It is not intended to be a comprehensive study of the concepts and principles of those disciplines that are usually drawn upon by the investigator to evaluate evidence collected and sent to the laboratory. There are a number of excellent works, written by experts in each of the respective fields, which go into much greater detail than found here. The reader is encouraged to draw on those resources for further information. The story and all its details are fictional, and any resemblance to the facts and events of an actual case is coincidental.

The Story

A number of perpetrators have entered a conspiracy to commit financial fraud, a form of white-collar crime. White-collar crime can be divided into two very broad categories: (1) illegal activities by a groups of people to fraudulently make money for themselves, and (2) activities by a group of people seeking to further the aims of their company or organization at the expense of others.

The perpetrators in this particular case are trying to make money for themselves and to fund other illegal activities, such as drug dealing, smuggling high-tech equipment, money laundering, etc. Their plan is to obtain or make counterfeit cards, checks, and identification documents (ID) necessary to further their operation. They and their members and their "mules" use counterfeit documents to perpetrate their fraudulent schemes. "Mule" refers to an individual enlisted by the organization to use the counterfeit documents; mules keep some of the money for themselves, but give most of it back to those sponsoring them.

The production and use of high-quality counterfeit documents are critical to the success of these operations. To start their operation, the perpetrators need seed documents. How and where do they get these counterfeit documents? They know Southeast Asia has long been a source of excellent counterfeit cards and IDs, but today high-quality counterfeit documents can be made anywhere. With the advent of computer graphic technology and user-friendly software, it is possible for anyone having a basic knowledge of computers to create their own counterfeit documents.

Many counterfeit cards and IDs are made in the United States and Canada and used within their boundaries or smuggled into other countries. Historically, however, the better quality documents have originated in Southeast Asia or are made by criminal organizations having roots there. The most comprehensive study on this subject was carried out by Detective Chief Inspector John Newton, of the Metropolitan Police Service, London (see his report entitled "Organised 'Plastic' Counterfeiting"[1]). He traveled around the world collecting information on the individuals who had been arrested, the criminal organizations to which they belonged, and the routes they used to transport their counterfeit cards. He also collected forensic information developed from the linking of the counterfeit cards and combined all the information he had collected into this one report.

Criminal organizations from Southeast Asia and other areas are still producing high-quality counterfeit documents using commercially available computer graphic and printing systems. Before the switch to high-technology equipment, conventional printing processes such as offset and screenprinting were used extensively in the fabrication of counterfeit cards and IDs. These printing processes are still being used by some counterfeiters and will be for years to come.

How should an investigator consider a counterfeit document? For investigative purposes, the document first should be considered in its entirety based on those things that can be seen without a close examination. Second, the document should be considered as the sum of its parts and each part should be carefully examined.

Forensically, the counterfeit document must be considered exactly the same way. First, the characteristics of the entire document, such as the denomination of a piece of currency or the program and issuer of a payment card, etc., are considered, then the more subtle characteristics of each individual part of the document — printing processes, embossing, defect analysis, etc. — and how the whole was fabricated. The fabrication process and resulting defects in each process must be determined and cataloged for linkage purposes.

If the document is a check fabricated at a single site using the printing processes requiring negatives, screens, etc., then all the checks manufactured using these common components should have the same common source characteristics. When these characteristics are compared to other checks of the same kind from a different source, the identifying characteristics should be different.

A genuine or counterfeit payment card or ID usually consists of multiple components, each having different sources. For example, typical components of a payment card and many IDs are

- Base material (i.e., the plastic, paper, etc.)
- Printed information on the base material and characteristic features resulting from the printing process used to make each part of the document
- Inks or other substances used to make the document
- Optical variable device (OVD) and its characteristics
- Embossed information, special embossed logos, and identification of the machine or punch and die set used to emboss the card
- Encoding on the magnetic stripe, etc.
- Signature panel material

Each component of the document has evidentiary value that can provide the investigator with significant common-source information but only after a forensic analysis and linking of those common characteristics. By knowing which components have a common source, the investigator can link cards and investigations that otherwise may have no connection.

A counterfeiter, just like a genuine manufacturer, does not purchase all of the items he uses to manufacture these documents from a single source. They both obtain supplies, graphics, equipment, materials, etc. from many different sources. These sources change over time, and as they do each change will affect the final product, a fact that must be considered by the investigator and forensic examiner.

An important item is the equipment used to make the counterfeits. A forensic analysis of equipment can provide evidence to establish what equipment was used in the fabrication of specific cards. Some examples of the equipment used to make cards include:

- Fabrication molds and holders
- Laminators
- Computers, software, and printers
- Printing screens, negatives, and blankets
- Embossers and encoders
- Typewriters and ribbons

All of these items are easy to obtain in the commercial marketplace.

As discussed above, individual card components are examined and, where possible, linked to determine whether they have a common source. This examination is done on the documents themselves and does not require the presence or forensic examination of the equipment used to make them. This examination is based on a comprehensive forensic analysis of the documents, the fabrication methods, common defects resulting from those methods, and the equipment used. The result of this examination can indicate that certain features on two or more documents come from a common source or were made using the same piece of equipment.

Anyone can purchase the technology and equipment to make counterfeit documents, because the same technology and equipment are used to make documents for legitimate purposes. The equipment can be purchased at office and graphic art supply stores, over the Internet, from a catalog, and occasionally from the equipment manufacturer. Criminal organizations purchase the equipment they need using counterfeit checks, or they steal it from businesses using it for legitimate purposes. Some criminals have stolen complete ID systems, preprinted stock, and other supplies for making IDs from state Department of Motor Vehicles (DMV) offices around the nation.

To get started, criminals also use established networks to obtain counterfeit cards, checks, and ID from Southeast Asia and elsewhere. Using these seed supplies allows them to purchase the equipment they need to make their own counterfeit documents. After starting with their seed supplies, they may purchase copies of graphics from other counterfeiters, or use some of the original counterfeit documents as models for making their own documents. They may use only portions of the original counterfeit graphics as a model and change others on the documents they are making. This intermixing of common and different parts of counterfeit documents is commonplace. That is why investigators and forensic examiners must consider any counterfeit document in its entirety and as a sum of its individual parts.

There are some decisions that the leaders of criminal organization must make before they order their counterfeit products. Counterfeit payment cards and IDs are available in many stage of completeness. If the criminals in our story have access to an embossing machine and encoder, they have the basic equipment necessary to personalize a plastic card having a magnetic stripe.

If they purchase counterfeit MasterCard, Visa, and Novus cards and a few others who use special embossed logos, they need special these embossed program and issuer logos to emboss the card. For example, the Visa embossed logo (known as a "Flying V") is produced by an oversized punch-and-die set. Because the amount of displacement pressure necessary to emboss this character in the card stock is greater than that required for the OCR and alpha-numeric characters, this oversized punch-and-die set will not work in all embossing machines. Counterfeit punch-and-dies of these embossed logos are available, or pre-embossed logo cards can also be obtained, in which case all that is needed to complete the personalization process is to emboss the card with the account number and other cardholder information.

If the criminal organization in our story has sufficient working capital and their embossing machine will support an oversized punch-and-die set, they can have a custom-made counterfeit logo punch-and-die set manufactured to fit their embosser. In addition to the embosser, they need an encoder, access to counterfeit optical variable devices (OVDs), hot-stamp equipment, laminators, etc. Most important of all, they need account information to personalize the cards. The account information, primarily the number, is referred to as the access device.

How does the criminal obtain account numbers and cardholder information?

- Friends or other members of the group who have access to the information (i.e., a person planted inside the bankcard approval center) can supply credit histories, account numbers, etc.
- A collusive merchant, for a price, will electronically tap his card reader and obtain account information from a genuine card magnetic stripe. He may double swipe a card, once for payment and a second time possibly through

another card reader connected to a computer. The information is stored in a database and then passed on. This process of reading and collecting the encoded information from a card's magnetic stripe is called "skimming". There are numerous variations of this criminal scheme, but the common characteristic they all have is to collect the data on the magnetic stripe of a genuine card. After the information is compromised, it is used to encode another card that can be used by an unauthorized individual to obtain cash advances or buy goods and services.

- Some criminals surf the Internet and find software programs useful in generating usable account numbers. There have even been sites giving away access device information.

If the criminals can obtain skimmed information from a card magnetic stripe, they have what they need for most transactions. Except for the personal identification number (PIN), the skimmed information provides account information and security codes necessary to access an account. If the use of the card requires a PIN, they will have to get that number from a different source. The actual PIN number is not encoded on the card magnetic stripe. It may have an encoded PIN offset that operates in conjunction with the PIN number, but the actual PIN number is not encoded on the magnetic stripe. Skimming of magnetic stripe information is a significant problem because it provides criminals with so much usable information.

Counterfeit checks, like payment cards and ID, are made using either conventional printing technology or computer graphics. While a model document would be nice to have, it is not always necessary to have it to make a counterfeit. The same is true for cards and IDs. There are so many different document formats used that it is impossible for merchants to know what any particular genuine document looks like. There are published reference booklets that provide merchants with information about the design of driver's licenses and some other IDs issued by various governmental organizations; however, because most of these books are abridged versions of more detailed references, they do not contain complete information.

A counterfeiter can use software programs such as Adobe Illustrator® or Coral Draw® to create the graphics he needs to make counterfeit checks, cards, and IDs. If he uses computer graphics to create documents, he will need a thermal mass/dye printer to print payment cards and IDs and various other high-quality printers to print counterfeit checks, etc. If he uses the correct printer, he will be able to make counterfeit checks with machine-readable magnetic ink optical character recognition numbers. Purchasing check safety paper is no problem, because it is available in office supply stores. If he has some of this basic equipment, he is ready to create counterfeit documents. Using these counterfeit documents, he can purchase other equipment necessary to make a more sophisticated counterfeit card and ID.

The criminals in our story have made some mistakes. Some of them are arrested while using counterfeit documents. At the time of their arrest, investigators seize the documents they have in their possession and take them to the laboratory for analysis. The process for submitting documents to the laboratory for analysis is described later in the chapter.

What Is Forensics?

The New Britannica-Webster Dictionary defines forensics as "belonging to, used in, or suitable to courts of law or to public discussion and debate."[2] *Webster's* defines forensics as "1. pertaining to or used in courts of law or in public debate; 2. adapted or suited to argumentation; rhetorical; 3. of, pertaining to, or involved with forensic medicine or forensic anthropology: forensic laboratories; ...5. <forensics> a department of forensic medicine, as in a police laboratory."[3]

How many forensic disciplines are there? Too many to list them all here. The American Academy of Forensic Sciences (AAFS), one of the largest and most respected professional organizations of forensic scientists, is divided into the following committees:

- Criminalistics
- Engineering Sciences
- General
- Jurisprudence
- Odontology
- Pathology/Biology
- Physical Anthropology
- Psychiatry and Behavioral Science
- Questioned Documents
- Toxicology

Within each committee, there are numerous specialties. In addition to the AAFS, there are other highly respected professional organizations of forensic scientists — for example, the International Association of Identification (IAI), which has some of the same disciplines as the AAFS plus a Fingerprint section, and the Canadian Society of Forensic Scientists. These professional societies serve as forums for forensic scientists to meet and discuss areas of mutual interest and are a source of continuing education for each represented discipline.

What Is a Forensic Scientist?

The forensic scientist applies his knowledge and training in a specialized scientific field to the examination of evidence, reports his findings and conclusions to the investigator and court, and when necessary gives testimony in court as an expert witness. His specialized knowledge in a scientific field may have been obtained from a formal college education in the sciences of medicine, chemistry, physics, etc. He may even have an advanced degree (Master's or doctorate) in his field. However, the successful completion of a college program, even a Master's degree program in forensic science, does not automatically qualify the graduate to work and testify in court as a forensic expert in his field. After completing his college work, the forensic scientist receives several additional years of training in an apprenticeship program learning how to apply his formal educational knowledge with new skills on how to examine evidence.

Some forensic scientists work in specialized areas for which there is no college or university degree program. For example, a one- or two-semester course in questioned documents, fingerprints, tool-marks, etc. is not sufficient to meet the professional standards necessary for qualifying in court as a expert. There are survey college courses and short seminar programs offered in these areas, but the completion of these also is not sufficient to qualify as an expert. Typically, the apprenticeship program for one of these forensic disciplines is 3 or more years of post-college work in an acceptable apprenticeship program under the direct supervision of certified forensic scientists. If the laboratory is accredited by the American Society of Crime Lab Directors (ASCLAD), the apprentice learns and practices daily the proper procedures for securing, handling, recording, and tracking evidence submitted to the laboratory for analysis.

Where does the forensic examiner work? Typically, in the laboratory and when necessary at the crime scene. Some forensic laboratories specialize in handling documentary evidence (i.e., the Secret Service Forensic Laboratory), and there are numerous broad-based police laboratories, such as the FBI laboratory, which handle a variety of evidence including questioned documents. These broad-based laboratories utilize the talents of a more diverse staff of forensic disciplines.

Historically, the forensic laboratory was referred to as a police laboratory staffed by laboratory investigators: "The function of the laboratory in police work is the scientific examination of physical evidence. Usually the purpose of this examination is to determine the manner in which a crime was committed to connect a suspect with the crime or to aid in establishing the identity of the criminal."[4]

If the forensic scientist is in private practice, as many are, he usually has a laboratory in which to conduct examinations as a part of the service he offers. The forensic examiner in private practice is frequently retained by the defense to verify the procedures, techniques, methodology, and findings of the government or police laboratory scientist. In either situation, the laboratory should be equipped with the necessary state-of-the-art analytical equipment for the forensic examiner to conduct the required examinations.

While evidence is usually examined in a laboratory, there are occasions when the forensic examiner leaves the laboratory environment, goes to the crime scene, and assists crime-scene technicians in the collection and preservation of evidence. This usually occurs when only the forensic examiner has the specialized knowledge and skills to conduct the preliminary examinations at the crime scene. Such situations are rare for the police laboratory examiner and rarer still for the private examiner.

The collection and preservation of evidence at a crime scene are usually done by an investigator and/or crime-scene technician who has received specialized training in the recognition, collection, and preservation of evidence. What are the usual steps followed at a crime scene? They include, but are not limited to:[5]

- Approaching the crime scene with great caution so as not to disturb any possible evidence

- Securing and protecting all evidence contained at the crime scene
- Conducting a preliminary survey of the scene
- After completion of the preliminary survey, determining where evidence is likely to be found and finding it
- Preparing a narrative description of the crime scene (including specifics about the condition of the crime scene)
- Photographing the crime scene (a photographic record of the crime scene including the evidence, its location, and condition at the crime scene is imperative for record purposes)
- Making sketches or drawings of the crime scene to establish a permanent record to support the photograph record
- Performing a search and detailed recording of what evidence was found, where it was found, who found it, and what disposition was made of it
- Final surveying of the crime scene before the scene is released (the crime-scene technician and investigator usually have only one chance to collect evidence, so thoroughness in their work is essential)

Frequently the crime-scene technicians are in charge of the crime scene. No one enters or leaves the scene without their permission, and nothing can be disturbed or removed until they say it can be. Preservation of the crime scene is critical to ensure the best possible chances of reconstructing the criminal events that have taken place and recover evidence of those events.

The crime-scene technician initially processes evidence as it is uncovered at the scene, records what and where evidence was found, and properly packages it for transfer to the laboratory. Some technicians have an extensive forensic background even though they are not forensic scientists. Crime-scene technicians are better able to understand what the laboratory scientist does than the investigator. The technician has this knowledge because he and the scientist work closely with each other.

In our story, some of the criminals were apprehended, searched, and found to have in their possession a number of counterfeit checks, cards, and IDs in many different names. In most cases like this, the arresting officer or investigator finds the evidence. Here he assumes the role of crime-scene technician. In this role he must have the basic knowledge and skills of a crime-scene technician. The responsibility is solely his for ensuring that he does not contaminate the evidence, that accurate records are made of what and where evidence was found, and that the evidence is properly packaged for transport to the laboratory. If he fails in any of these areas, the case could be dismissed.

How Can a Forensic Examiner Provide Assistance?

The forensic examiner provides assistance to the investigator and the investigation in many different ways. First, as we have said, he must work closely with the investigator to help him understand the needs of the laboratory just as he must understand the needs of the investigator. How is this accomplished? By:

- The forensic examiner taking part in the basic training of the investigator at the police academy
- Conducting personal tours of the laboratory for investigators
- Sitting down with the investigator after the forensic examination is complete to explain the examinations performed on the evidence submitted and the meaning of the report results; the forensic examiner can answer questions the investigator may have concerning why the examinations were performed and how the results of those examinations can assist in his investigation
- Building a mutual professional working relationship between forensic examiner and investigator so neither one feels threatened by the other

Both the forensic examiner and the investigator must understand the limits imposed by the law and the application of science as it applies to the examined evidence in each case. Establishing a professional respect for the training and abilities of the other is critical.

Back to our example case, we will assume the apprehension of the criminals in our story took place in a bank. The teller and branch manager recognized that the documents presented were not genuine or were certainly suspicious. The bank manager contacted the police, who responded quickly to the call. After their arrival at the bank, the police detained and searched the suspects. During the search, the investigator found additional documents, checks, cards, and IDs. He suspected that they, too, were counterfeit and properly recorded all of the evidence, preserving it by placing it in protective envelopes or bags. Our suspects were arrested at the scene and transported to the police station for further questioning.

At the station, the investigator stopped by the Questioned Document Laboratory to consult with the Questioned Document Examiner on duty. They reviewed the seized evidence and completed the necessary paper work to submit the evidence for examination. The investigator learned from the examiner what else he may need to ensure that they have the best evidence available for examination purposes. This type of consultation between investigator and scientist should be the norm rather than the exception. The examiner provides assistance to the investigator, not because he is an advocate for any position, but because his only interest is in having the best available evidence for examination.

The forensic scientist must be impartial at all times. The examiner cannot do anything that will be interpreted as his favoring either side or being influenced by information developed during the course of the investigation. If the examiner is not impartial, his work could result in a mistake being made that results in casting suspicion on an innocent person. A forensic scientist who is not impartial or who demonstrates the least bit of favoritism toward one side or the other will not have the respect of those for whom he works or his peers.

Identifying the wrong person or the equipment used to commit a crime is an intolerable result. Mistakes have been made and do occur, in spite of all the checks and balances in the system. The ultimate goal is to have no mistakes, but because the ultimate is not a realistic possibility, the more realistic goal is to keep mistakes to an absolute minimum.

Forensic Specialists Most Frequently Used in a Financial Crime Case

Documents are the evidence items usually developed in white-collar crime cases such as financial fraud. Equipment such as computers, scanners, printers, magnetic stripe readers/encoders, software, etc. are generally found in either or both the counterfeiting or finishing plants. For example, the counterfeit payment card is fabricated at a counterfeiting plant, and from there it may go to a finishing plant where the following additions to the card are made:

- Access information, account number, cardholder name, special embossed logos, etc. are embossed and data encoded on the magnetic stripe of the card or ID.
- OVDs, overlays, signature panels, etc. are applied to the card or ID.
- The person who will be using the ID is photographed, or they bring or send a photograph to the finishing plant, where it is attached to the ID.

In the case of our criminals, they were buying, making, and using documents for their criminal activity. Those arrested were mules having completed counterfeit documents in their possession. In this type of case, the forensic scientists most frequently examining this type of evidence are Forensic Questioned Document Examiners and Fingerprint Specialists. Another specialist that may be retained for assistance is the Forensic Ink Chemist (FIC). When forensic ink analysis is required, as it sometimes is, a specialist in forensic ink chemistry conducts the examinations and tries to answer questions posed by the investigator. Depending upon the questions asked and the available evidence, he may be able to render a conclusive determination. Occasionally a "yes" or "no" answer is not possible. There are many other forensic disciplines; however, the remainder of this chapter assumes that only the Forensic Questioned Document Examiner and Fingerprint Specialist are called upon to examine evidence in this case. A brief discussion of the work of a Forensic Ink Chemist is provided later in this chapter.

Sometimes mules know the location of the counterfeiting or finishing plant. If they provide this information to the police after their arrest and the police obtain a search warrant to execute a raid on the plant, a Forensic Computer Specialist (FCS) should also be a part of the crime-scene team. Their role is to ensure the integrity of the computer systems and data found at the crime scene. Because computer crime is such a highly technical area, it will not be addressed any further at this time.

The Forensic Questioned Document Examiner

What exactly is a Forensic Questioned Document Examiner? Ordway Hilton describes the profession as follows: "The profession of examiners of questioned documents grew out of the needs of the courts for assistance in interpreting evidence relating to the preparation and subsequent treatment of documents."[6] He goes on to say, "The reader must recognize that a document examiner is trained not only to examine various elements of the document but also to consider the whole document. He is concerned with the identification of the factors which make up the document and the detection of manipulation or falsification."[7]

Well, what *is* a document? Alwyn Cole defines a document this way: "A document is defined as a record of the thoughts of men, by means of any symbol, on any material substance. You know that a definition is supposed to give the limits of a thing but a document defies limitation. A definition that includes the element '...a record of the thoughts of men...' is indeed broad. These words show that the study of documents has no real limits other than those that affect mankind generally."[8]

Precisely because the definition is so broad, it is only through constant study and experimentation by the examiner that he is able to keep up with changes in his profession. Training takes on two forms: formal study and observation and experimentation. Observation and experimentation, for example, provide ways for the examiner to learn how people write naturally or disguise their writing, how to conduct ink studies, how documents are altered, or how to examine and identify embossing machines or new printing processes. Observation and experimentation are very critical in the training of an examiner or any other forensic scientist.

What Type of Examinations Does the Forensic Document Examiner Perform?

The examiner inspects documents to try to determine the following.

Identification of the Writer of Handwritten or Hand-Printed Material

The handwritten material may consist of extended writings, signatures, numerals, or even marks — "X" — representing signatures. The style of writing may be Roman, Chinese, Greek, Arabic, etc. The principles of handwriting/hand-printing identification are beyond the scope of this text and are not covered. The reader is referred to published texts on the subject written by competent, qualified, and ethical examiners of handwriting if they wish to learn more about this subject.

Individual handwriting characteristics are now being digitized and stored in a computer database. The Germans developed a system called the Forensic Information System for Handwriting (FISH) that uses characteristics of certain letters and other handwriting features as part of the database. The German government shared this technology with the U.S. Secret Service's Questioned Document Laboratory in Washington, D.C., where it is currently in use. FISH is designed for use with extended handwritten text problems. At this time, it is not being used with signature or similar short-text handwriting problems.

Let us assume that John Jones has provided handwriting samples on a prior occasion that were digitized and stored in a FISH database. Now Jones is suspected of writing a threatening letter which is in the possession of law enforcement. The investigator, after receiving the letter, refers it to the laboratory for analysis. The examiner conducts a preliminary examination of the letter to determine whether it is suitable for searching in the FISH system and, if so, which handwriting characteristics are entered so the database can be queried for possible writers. After entering the new data, the database is queried for possible suspects. Once these suspects are identified, the examiner performs a handwriting comparison examination to determine if one of the suspects wrote the questioned letter. The specimen writing used by the examiner for this examination is on file in the laboratory. The writer of the letter may not be of record.

In rare instances, a writer is able to change his writing style and its identifiable features sufficiently so that the new letter cannot be associated with any of the current known writers, himself included.

Identification of Business Machine Impressions To Link Documents

Some examples of business machine impressions the examiner can identify are typewriters, check protectors, printers, plastic card embossers, rubber and steel stamps, paper cutter blades, die-cutters, etc. Business machine impressions, such as typewriters, have long been one of the more complex examinations for the examiner. Part of the reason for this is that there are many different machines having similar type designs. Today, this is even more true. With the advent of computer printers and the different technologies they use, identifying a particular printer based on the type of font design and its characteristics is almost impossible. Type designs and point size are established by software bit maps and not by a piece of engraved or cast metal that makes contact with a ribbon and paper. Computer type characteristics are selected from a menu that is part of the software and not by replacing a piece of type or escapement component in the typewriter.

Examination of the impressions of typewriters, printers, or rubber stamps is typically an inspection of two-dimensional characteristics (character height and width).[9] Check protectors and some steel stamp impressions have three-dimensional characteristics (character height, width, and depth), but usually they are two-dimensional impressions.

Embosser type, both the punch and die, requires a three-dimensional examination. The punch is similar to Figure 1 and the die is usually a mirror of the punch, but with the type-design recessed in the body so the pair mate with each other. Embosser punch-and-dies, die-cutters, and cutting blades leave three-dimensional images, striations, and defects, in the material. It is the unique pattern and nature of the combination of the residual features left by these devices that make them identifiable.

Figure 1 shows a piece of type with its component parts identified. There is a chip in the typeface and bevel and a defect on the bevel surface. If this is a piece of typewriter type, only the typeface makes contact with a ribbon placed between the typeface and paper. If Figure 1 were a piece of embossing type, the typeface, bevel, and

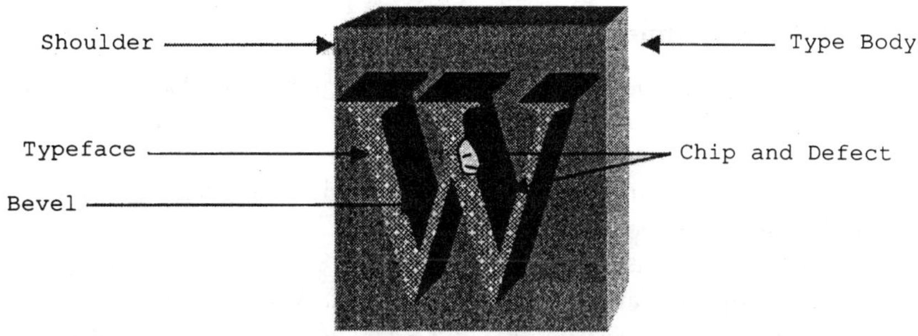

Figure 1. A piece of type with its component parts identified. There is a chip in the typeface and bevel, and a defect on the bevel surface. If this is a piece of typewriter type, only the typeface makes contact with a ribbon placed between the typeface and paper. If Figure 1 were a piece of embossing type, the typeface, bevel, and frequently the shoulder make contact with the plastic card surface. The detail characteristics of the chip and defects on the bevel would be recorded in the plastic and remain there after the punch was removed.

frequently the shoulder make contact with the plastic card surface. The detail characteristics of the chip and defects on the bevel would be recorded in the plastic and remain there after the punch was removed.

When an examiner conducts a typewriter examination — a two-dimensional examination — he is usually dealing with the image left only by the typeface. If the typeface has a chip, as in Figure 1, the outline of the chipped area may be found on the inked image remaining on the paper surface after the typeface and ribbon are removed.

If a chip or defect is present on either or both an embossing machine punch and die, when they are removed from the surface residual impressions remain in the surface material. Because there is so much detail remaining in the embossed surface, it is easier to identify this three-dimensional image than it is to examine and identify a two-dimensional image. More information on this topic is available in the article described in Note 7.

Document Alteration

Document alteration can be a significant problem for the examiner. He can usually determine whether a document is altered, and if so how the alteration was made. Occasionally, he can determine what information was on the document before the alteration. The document may be paper — such as a business agreement, payroll book, check, an entry in a journal — or it may be a plastic card having an altered embossed account number or cardholder information.

The use of sophisticated equipment such as infrared and ultraviolet light imaging, electrostatic detection systems to view indentations in the document, and chemical analysis of ink and paper are but a few of the methods available to the examiner. A great deal of literature on the equipment and techniques to use them is available and the reader should refer to that literature for more detailed information.

Genuineness of Documents

The use of counterfeit documents is increasing significantly. Passports, driver's licenses, and other IDs, as well as payment cards and negotiable instruments such as stocks and bonds, are just a few examples of the type of documents being counterfeited. Many document issuers are switching to plastic cards because they are convenient and have been widely accepted by the public.

Occasionally, a document's genuineness can be determined even if a genuine specimen document is not available or does not exist. While it is desirable to have a specimen available for comparison purposes, there are occasions when no genuine exists. A counterfeit payment card purportedly issued by a nonexistent financial institution and a driver's license with an Ohio front and a Virginia back are but two examples. Sometimes the entire payment card or ID is created without having any model to compare it with. Nevertheless, where no specimen is available, it is still possible to determine forensically that the document being examined is counterfeit.

Necessary Examiner Knowledge

Some of the topics and technology for which an examiner must have a working knowledge include the following.

Writing Systems

If the examination involves handwriting or hand-printing identification, the examiner must have some knowledge of the different handwriting systems the suspects may have learned to write. The basic principle of handwriting identification is that there must be complete agreement in all features of writing important for identification with no significant or fundamental differences other than those differences or dissimilarities resulting from the normal variation present in the natural writing of the person. A significant or fundamental difference can be the absence of an unusual feature, a difference resulting from the use of extreme disguise, one that is unaccountable or unexplained, or one that is simply irreconcilable.

Differences or dissimilarities resulting from normal variation are caused by the fact that a human being is not a machine and is not capable of reproducing the exact same movements repetitively; therefore, some normal variation in all of the qualities and features of an individual's writing is to be expected.

The examiner must be able to determine which handwriting features should receive the greatest weight for identification purposes. By being familiar with handwriting systems and features written by many writers, he is able to determine which features meet the criteria. There are two kinds of features: class and individual. Class features are those derived from the general style to which the handwriting conforms[10] and are the result of the writing system and other factors surrounding what the writer learned as a child. They may also be the result of features found in a large number of different writers writing. Because such features are common to a large group of writers, they have only a limited amount of significance in handwriting identification. Individual features of writing have been introduced into the handwriting, consciously or unconsciously, by the writer.[10] These features may be unique, unusual, or rare and usually are found in the writing of a particular person. Because of their rarity, they are more important for identification purposes.

It is the combination of these class and individual features in sufficient quantity that will lead the examiner to conclude that two writings are of common authorship. How many are required? There is no set number required by any competent, qualified, and ethical examiner, certifying board, or technical organization. That is why the requirement for an identification is worded the way it is.

Writing Instruments

There are many different writing instruments, and each has its own unique characteristics when used on different surfaces. Some of these writing instruments are ballpoint pens, roller balls, fountain pens, pencils, crayons, or soft marking pencils. It is important for the examiner to be familiar with these different writing instruments, to know how they work and the markings they leave on different writing surfaces.

Inks

There are many different kinds of inks — writing inks, printing inks, etc. — which vary not only in color but also in their use and chemical formulation. These differences also apply to how each of the inks behaves on a different surface. The FIC receives special training to perform this work, but the examiner must have a basic working knowledge of inks to recognize when the service of an ink chemist is required.

Correction Fluid

Correction fluids are solvents used to remove or bleach ink so it will not be seen on the paper or writing surface. Different solvents react differently to ink formulations, chemicals in the paper, etc. Solvents that are a mixture of common household chemicals, commercial ink eradicators purchased from a store, or even uncommon chemicals such as brake fluid, etc. have been used to remove or bleach writing ink. The examiner should have an understanding of some of these chemicals and their reactions.

Correction fluid has been called the secretary's best friend and is frequently used to cover over typed or written material or an incorrect entry or to smooth out paper fiber disturbances resulting from mechanical abrasion, etc. If a document is altered using correction fluid, the examiner must know how to remove it without damaging the information under it or how to make the correction fluid translucent so he can see what is written or typed under it. Much work has been done in the area of developing freezing techniques to remove or make correction fluid translucent and micro-manipulation techniques to remove the correction fluid from the paper surface. Micro-manipulation is the process of physically removing the dried correction

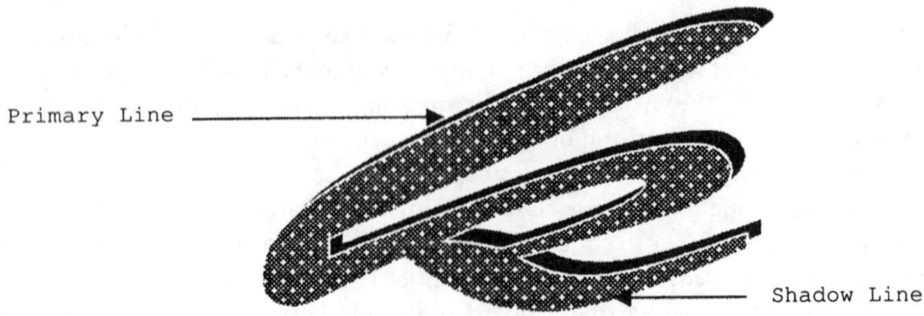

Figure 2. Effect of the ball housing of a pen creating a secondary line on NCR paper. The same effect can be found, but as an indentation, on a sheet of paper. If this effect is not properly evaluated, the writing may be mistaken for an indented outline tracing. A great deal of caution is necessary in the evaluation of this or any feature of a document.

fluid from the document's surface without damaging or destroying the material beneath it. Recovery of the material beneath correction fluid is the primary goal of this examination.

Copies and Copiers

There are many different types of material and processes used to make copies of documents: carbon and non-carbon (NCR®) paper, multiple copier printers, photocopiers, etc. Each has its own unique properties and challenges for the examiner. It is important for the examiner to be able to recognize what type of copy he is dealing with, how it is made, and whether it can be altered. Each type of process offers its own set of problems and cautions. For example, when a writer signs NCR® paper holding a writing instrument at too steep an angle to the paper surface, the following can occur: The ball housing of the pen drags on the paper as the writer is writing, which sometimes results in an indented shadow line on the original document and a dark line on the copies paralleling and intersecting the primary writing line as in Figure 2. This figure illustrates the effect of a ball pen housing creating a secondary line on a NCR® paper copy. The same effect can be found, but as an indentation, on a sheet of paper. If this effect is not properly evaluated, the writing may be mistaken for an indented outline tracing. A great deal of caution is necessary in the evaluation of this or any feature of a document.

The shadow line appears as an outline following and intersecting with the primary line. The assumption is made here that the writer of the material in Figure 2 is righthanded. Typically, with righthanded writers, this shadow line will be on the right side of a downstroke and on the left side of an upstroke. Even though Figure 2 does not show this phenomenon exactly, it does illustrate that a shadow line can be present on both the original and a copy, and when it is present, its cause must not be misinterpreted. The effect of this dragging, as mentioned above, has on occasion been misinterpreted as evidence of a tracing, which it is not. The shadow effect can be different for some lefthanded writers.

Occasionally, a similar effect will occur when the writing is on a sheet of paper. The presence of an indented shadow line on a piece of paper could suggest the writing is the result of an indented outline tracing and such an interpretation of the evidence may be incorrect.

If a photocopy is the subject of the examination by the examiner, it is sometimes necessary to first determine what copier process was used so he will know how to interpret the evidence. He also needs to know what effects the copying process will have on the copied material. Not all inks copy well; for instance, some blue ballpoint pen inks, when copied, result in very poor images.

The size of the original material may not be the same as the copy. The size and details of the original information can very significantly from the original depending upon its location on the page and other factors. Understanding the copying process and what can happen to the image during it is important for the examiner. If it is necessary to identify the copier process and copy machine, it may be necessary to perform a chemical analysis of the toners. The individual doing this work should have a background in chemistry.

Paper

What is it? What are its properties? Are all papers alike? The study of paper is also a specialized area and the examiner is not expected to be an expert in paper analysis. He should, however, have:

- A working knowledge of how paper is made and its properties
- A working knowledge of the different kinds of paper, their uses, and how they react in different situations and environments
- A working knowledge of writing papers and how they react to writing inks, erasures, folding, solvents, etc.

The examiner should have a basic knowledge of paper because in his work he may be asked, for example, to determine the date or period of time when a document or one of its components was produced or changed.

Mechanical Devices

Documents are created using various mechanical devices such as typewriters, check writers, computer printers, mimeographs and other duplication machines, plastic and metal embossing machines, etc. Each machine has characteristics that make it identifiable. The examiner must know what the characteristics are and how to properly evaluate their significance when he sees them. This is not an easy task. Considerable time is spent studying and developing skills and techniques necessary to examine documents produced on any of these or the many other machines that can be used to make a document.

Hand-Recording Equipment

Machines are not the only devices used to produce markings on documents. Rubber and steel stamps, seals, authenticating devices, and others are regularly used to authenticate a document or an entry on the document. Each has its own unique set of class and individual characteristics that make it identifiable. Rubber and steel stamps can have dents or chips in the typeface that will produce a void in that character on the paper or other substance. Seals and cachets may be counterfeit and placed on the document to give it the appearance of being genuine.

Printing Processes

The types of documents that examiners are now examining require a comprehensive understanding of printing technology. This is especially true for plastic card documents such as IDs and payment cards. The use of printed plastic is rapidly becoming the preferred method of creating financial and identification documents of all types. In the future, plastic card documents will be a major component of the Forensic Document Examiner's work. Paper documents such as personal and business checks or birth certificates and other counterfeit paper documents are being sent to the laboratory for analysis with greater frequency.

The characteristics of various printing processes on plastic and paper can be very different. The examiner must understand printing processes so he can give proper weight to any characteristics or defects found in the printing he may encounter. The significance of any defect can be a function of the specific printing method used and the defects occurring as a result of the printing process. For example, thermal-mass printing (TMP) is used to print material on specially coated paper and PVC plastic cards. The examiner should know how it works, what factors affect the printing process, and how to determine whether the printed material on different cards may have been done on the same or similar printers.

Types of Examinations Performed by Forensic Ink Chemists

The Forensic Ink Chemist (FIC) is a specialist in the analysis of ink. Forensic ink analysis is both a nondestructive and semi-destructive examination made to determine the physical/chemical profile of the ink. This profile consists of optical and dye/pigment content properties. Inks analyzed include writing, printing, stamp pad, and typewriter ribbon inks and photocopy toners. An FIC compares inks to determine similarities or differences. If a collection of reference standards exists, an FIC can compare a particular ink against this collection to determine the source (manufacturer or, in the case of writing inks, the date of first production). Finally, an FIC should be knowledgeable of, or be able to perform, relative age determination of writing inks.[11]

Occasionally, a question arises concerning ink entries on documents. The FIC is most frequently asked to:

- Determine the date an entry or signature was written by a writer
- Determine whether two ink entries were written with ink having the same formulation
- Determine whether several ink entries were written at or about the same time

Types of Examinations Performed by the Fingerprint Specialist

Fingerprint characteristics have been used for over 100 years as a reliable means of identification. A practitioner of this discipline is known as a Fingerprint Specialist (FS), but this title is misleading. Actually, the FS processes evidence for latent prints (i.e., finger-, palm-, or footprints) and compares suitable latent and specimen ink prints to determine whether they belong to the same person. The fingerprint is not the only part of the body that can be used to identify a person. Other biometric features of a person can have their own unique patterns of identifiable characteristics. A few examples of biometric identifiers include:

- Fingers, palms, feet, and toes, which have a unique combination of friction ridges
- The voice, which has a modulated pattern of sound waves
- The face, which has a unique combination of measurements (in brief, the image of the face is covered by a two-dimensional matrix which serves as a reference for measurements of components of the face, such as the distance between the eyes or from the eyes to the ear)
- Unique pattern of the eyes retina
- Handwriting of a person based on a set of unique movement characteristics

A detailed discussion of each of these and other biometric identifiers is beyond the scope of this text; however, a brief discussion of fingerprints follows to familiarize the reader with some concepts of this form of biometric identifier and how it applies to our case.

What is a latent print? A latent print is a hidden print that must be developed and recorded so it can be seen and compared. It usually becomes visible after the area where it is located is processed with chemicals or powders. After development, the formerly latent print is evaluated to determine whether it is suitable for comparison purposes and then it is photographed. Not all developed latent prints are suitable for identification purposes. Some prints, both inked and developed latents, are partial or fragmentary and frequently do not contain sufficient detail necessary for comparison purposes. Evidence is usually processed for latent print development when there is reason to believe it contains latent prints or when the surface is suitable for latent print development.

Many different processing methods are available to the FS. In recent years, new chemicals and processing methods have been developed and used which increase the probability of latent print development. Latent print processing can be divided into four general categories: chemical, powder, thin-film vacuum deposition, and special lighting. The method chosen depends on the type of item being processed (paper, plastic, metal, glass, etc.) and the experience of the examiner.

The FBI Identification Division is probably the best known fingerprint identification office in the world. It was established over 75 years ago when the FBI received approximately 810,188 fingerprint files, primarily from Leavenworth Penitentiary.[12] They now have over 250 million sets of prints in their file and receive over 34,000 additional sets of prints each day. To keep up with this vast number of prints, they have developed an automated fingerprint analysis system, the Integrated Automated Fingerprint Identification System (IAFIS), to replace the old card file system.

A number of other federal, state, and local police agencies have similar automated fingerprint information systems (AFISs). Many AFISs are connected together, allowing different police agencies to share their database information. They do this through written Memorandums of Understanding (MOU) authorizing the sharing of data. The reason for sharing this data is that criminals are mobile and it is imperative that law enforcement be able to identify a criminal as quickly as possible.

Fingerprints are identified by comparing friction ridge patterns in the latent and inked prints to determine whether the pattern is the same and that the details of the patterns are identical. Friction ridges are series of ridges, separated by corresponding depressions, in the skin found on the fingers, hands, toes, feet, etc. There are seven basic patterns of fingerprint friction ridges, usually named after their shape (see Figure 3):

1. Central Pocket Loop
2. Double Loop
3. Accidental
4. Plain Arch
5. Plain Whorl
6. Loop
7. Tented Arch

A friction ridge contains small pores that secrete perspiration, which remains behind after the removal of the ridge from the surface. The pattern left by the secreted perspiration mirrors the friction ridge characteristics on the finger, hand, toe, foot, etc. If there is no secretion from these pores, then ridge detail is not likely to be found on the touched surface. There is an exception, however. If the friction ridge is wet, greasy, or coated with some substance that will adhere to the ridges and ultimately on the touched surface, then the print can be developed and recorded for record and comparison purposes.

In addition to the ridge detail, the pores in the ridges can have their own identifiable characteristics. Their number, size, and location on the ridge are other identifiable characteristics. A more detailed discussion of fingerprint and pore identification can be found in recognized texts on the subject; the purpose here is simply to introduce the reader to some of the basic concepts associated with this form of biometric identification.

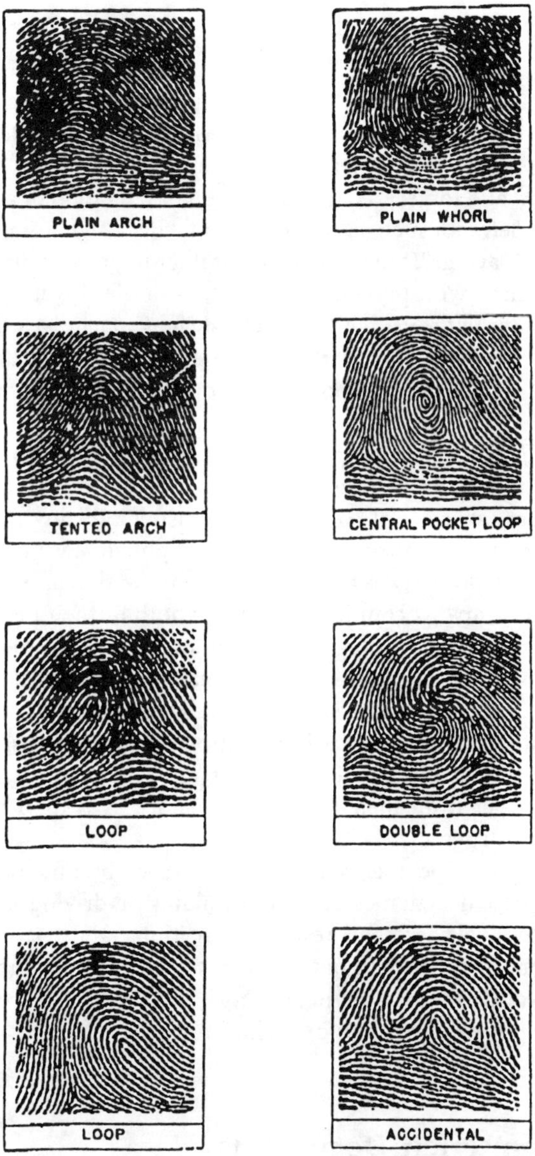

Figure 3. Illustrations of various fingerprint patterns.[13] The presence or existence of whorls in the finger impressions is used as the basis for the determination of the chief or primary classification. Each whorl appearing in any or all of the ten fingers has a certain arbitrary or fixed value. The addition of the values represented by such whorls and the indicatin of the total value are known as the primary classification. Illustrations of the whorl types which are the same as patterns having the figured value are shown on the right; illustrations of the other types are shown on the left. (Courtesy of Federal Bureau of Investigation, United States Department of Justice.)

Counterfeit Documents

What is a counterfeit? One definition is "an imitation intended to be passed off as genuine; forgery."[14] Wielandt describes a counterfeit as "the reproduction of a document, article, or security feature with the intent to deceive the close scrutiny of a qualified examiner" and forgery as "the replication or alteration of a document's data with the intent to defraud, such as check amount, check signature, and data."[15]

There is an old saying, "If man makes it, another man can counterfeit it." This is a significant statement with potentially serious, even life-threatening implications. Production of counterfeit consumer products, such as watches, clothes, or hardware items, is growing, and the cost to the world economy is staggering. The use of counterfeit hardware items such as bolts, rivets, or airplane parts jeopardizes people's lives daily.

Counterfeiting intellectual property such as music CDs, videotapes, or software is also a significant problem costing the public billions of dollars a year. The use of counterfeit software can corrupt computer systems by infecting them with viruses, and it deprives the user of realizing his full creative potential were he to use genuine software. Intellectual property represents the future and economic interest of its originator and his company; counterfeits deprive both of their deserved rewards.

Counterfeit and forged documents are another significant problem. Counterfeit currency, payment cards, or checks pose a threat to our country and the world's economic stability. Criminal organizations, such as the one in our story, use counterfeit payment documents, access device information obtained from skimming genuine card magnetic stripes, identification documents, etc. to perpetrate their fraud. Some of the money they get from their fraudulent operations is used to buy computer equipment, jewelry, drugs, etc.

False identification documents are frequently used by underage individuals to participate in restricted activities such as drinking or driving a car. They allow unauthorized individuals access to restricted locations, and terrorists use them to travel from country to country to obtain money and carry out their activities. The bombing of the World Trade Center in New York and the downing of the TWA flight over Scotland are but two examples of such terrorism.

How Are Counterfeit Documents Detected and What Can the Forensic Document Examiner Do with Them?

How are counterfeit documents detected? There are three levels of counterfeit detection. Wielandt describes them as follows:[16]

> *Level 1: In the first-line inspection, the document is checked without equipment. This concerns public security features like watermark, tactile intaglio printing,*

microprint, security threads, holograms, optically variable ink, and registered printing.

Level 2: In second-line inspection, the document is checked with simple tools by bank tellers, cashiers, and so on. These are more or less trained inspectors but no forensic specialists. Second-line security features are, for example, magnetic ink, bar codes, retroreflection, and luminescence.

Level 3: In third-line inspection, the document is investigated by forensic specialists with sophisticated means, most often in a laboratory environment or a dedicated inspection facility.

A casual inspection of a document performed at level one is usually limited to determining the presence or absence of public security features such as holograms, the feel of currency paper, security threads, watermarks, etc. The second level of inspection involves the use of features such as latent ultraviolet ink images, reading magnetic stripe information, signature association, etc. The third level of laboratory analysis involves detailed examination and analysis of every quality and feature of the document, comparing them with genuine features of the same type on specimen documents, when available. If specimen documents are not available because none exist, the laboratory examination results in a determination of why the document is counterfeit and its possible linkage to other similar documents.

Optical or nondestructive examinations and destructive instrumental analysis such as chemical analysis of paper, ink, plastic, etc. are performed at the third level. Reasons for conducting these examinations include:

- Forensic analysis of the documents for linking purposes
- Establishing possible sources of supplies for the materials and items used in their fabrication
- Providing information to investigators so they can locate and suppress the counterfeiting plant and the suppliers of the materials they used to create the documents

Some examples of the kinds of counterfeit documents examined include:

- Currency
- Payment cards
- Money orders
- Checks (i.e., personal, corporate, government, cashier)
- Identification documents and cards, birth certificates, passports, driver licenses
- Postage stamps
- Admission tickets (i.e., to concerts or sports activities)
- Airline and other transportation tickets
- Lottery tickets

Whether a counterfeit document is examined by the Forensic Document Examiner depends upon the initial establishment of its authenticity, with some degree of certainty, before it is given to him for a forensic examination. It depends also upon whether the result of his examination is required in the investigative phase of the case or for court purposes at the time of trial.

Because some counterfeit documents pose a more serious threat than others, their examination and evidentiary value cannot be overemphasized. Important documents such as passports and other IDs or payment cards should be submitted to the laboratory immediately for analysis and linkage to other similar documents.

The examination and linkage of counterfeit documents is part of the work of the Forensics Document Examiner, without whom making the connection between otherwise independent cases may never occur. With the laboratory and investigative information available to the investigator, it may be possible for the investigator to locate and suppress the numerous manufacturing operations and suppliers of materials necessary to produce the counterfeit document.

Many technologies and components are necessary to create a genuine document. Each technology and component is independent of the others, but when put together into one common whole they represent a secure document that is difficult to counterfeit. For example, a payment card consists of the following components:

- Card stock or plastic used for the core and overlay
- Printed program logo (i.e., Visa), which itself consists of the following parts: white background, fine-line printing around the outer edge of logo, blue bar, printed name, and gold bar.
- Printed background on a payment card

The genuine card uses a white core plastic, and the metallic background and graphics on the front and back surface are printed on the core in accordance with card program and issuer specifications. Counterfeit payment cards do not always have a white core plastic. Some use color (silver, gold, black, etc.) or metallic-impregnated plastic as stock material.

Identifying numbers or the words "Issue Date" or "Valid Thru" or similar words and phrases are not always "printed" on genuine cards. On many genuine cards, these words and some numbers are actually the core plastic surrounded by ink in the shape of the letter or numeral. If the background is screenprinted, ink is applied to the card surface by forcing it through open holes in a screen. Wherever the holes are blocked, no ink can be deposited on the card surface; therefore, the shapes of the letters and numerals for the card can be seen on the screen where the screen holes are blocked. No printing ink is applied to the surface of the plastic at these locations, so the printed material is actually the white core material surrounded by ink. The result is to create the effect of printed words or numbers.

Frequently on counterfeit cards these printed words and numerals are printed on top of the background using separate negatives or screens for each word, phrase, or set of numerals. This process allows the counterfeiter to use the same screen when printing many different card formats. For example, the words "Valid Thru" printed on a counterfeit Visa card can also be printed on a counterfeit MasterCard using the same screen.

The same words, phrases, and printed numerals are frequently used by different card programs and issuers. As seen in the above example, counterfeiters frequently use the same screen containing these common characteristics to print this information. They do this rather than produce a single screen each time they want to print a card.

When a card is made using computer graphics, each printed card component can be placed in a separate file that can be opened and used on any card. For example, various backgrounds, card names, issuer names, and logos can be used to make different cards. The process is very easy for those components common to a number of different cards such as Visa and MasterCard. This process is the same for both the legitimate manufacturer and counterfeiter using this technology.

In every counterfeit card examination, it must be determined whether all of the material on the card surface was printed at the same time or as separate items. For example, if the issuer name, validation dates, and bin number are printed in black, were they printed simultaneously using a single screen or were they printed on the cards as separate items? If sufficient defects are present in the printing of this material on two or more different program cards, it may be possible to link the cards.

Some documents have special printed security features such as medallion structures for three-dimensional effects, rainbow printing, complex guilloche patterns, etc., that are very difficult to duplicate. Defects in these features on counterfeit cards are very important for card linkage.

Another component of the card includes the printed material on the back of a card, excluding the printing of the signature panel. This printing on the back of the card should be located under the overlay and on the core plastic just as it is on the front of the card. On counterfeit cards the printing may be on the core, on top of the overlay, etc. Its location depends upon the fabrication method used by the counterfeiter.

The signature panel on the card can be a pre-printed hot stamp foil or can be screenprinted on top of the card overlay. The words or symbols used on the signature panel are normally printed on top of the panel base material. They may include the name of the issuer (i.e., Visa, MasterCard, or American Express) or symbolic logos identifying the card program or issuer. Some counterfeit cards produced using thermal-mass-transfer printing technology have these symbols and words printed on the overlay and covered by a printed translucent white stripe resembling the signature panel.

Some payment cards have an optical variable device (OVD) on the front and/or on the back of the card; this is a feature found on a number of European cards. Counterfeiters use OVD devices or some other means to create the impression that the card has an OVD because they want the card to pass the first line of inspection, but it is not necessary to have an exact replication of the OVD. OVDs can and are counterfeited routinely. Like the rest of the card, it is only necessary to have a passable product that can be used several times and then discarded.

If the counterfeit document (i.e., passports, plastic IDs, payment cards) consists of a number of separate components produced by different technologies and fabricating techniques, linking of these common components can be critical information for an investigator. As stated above, component linkage gives him information that can assist in locating and suppressing the manufacturers of the documents and the suppliers of the basic materials needed by the counterfeiter to make his product. Without such information, these separate manufacturers would be able to continue to make and sell their products to many different counterfeiters with little risk to themselves.

Counterfeiters use the same technology and equipment as those used by genuine document manufacturers. The examination of counterfeit and genuine documents requires the examiner to be familiar with these different technologies and to constantly learn about advances in those areas. If he does not keep up, he will possess outdated skills within a matter of a few years.

What Are the Investigator's Duties?

The investigator's duties can be generalized as follows. He must:

- Conduct a careful and impartial investigation, properly and accurately recording all statements and events.
- Collect, protect, and properly describe all evidence, recording it completely and accurately so there can be no confusion about what it is and where it was found at the crime scene.
- Submit all evidence for analysis to the laboratory in a timely fashion together with a clearly written description of the desired work (the examiner does not need, nor does he want to know, the background of the case, and he will ask the investigator any questions in a timely fashion).
- Evaluate the statements of witnesses, the forensic reports received from the laboratory, and all other evidence developed during the investigation to determine what most likely happened or occurred; the conclusion reached should naturally follow from the correct assessment and evaluation of all of this information.
- Write a clear report of his findings, citing all necessary references and presenting it to the proper court officer for action.

The investigator has a key role in the process of justice. He must take a collection of varying and often conflicting statements by witnesses, physical evidence developed at the crime scene, forensic reports of the physical evidence, and insight garnered from years of experience and determine whether there is sufficient evidence to present to an officer of the court for action. This is not an easy task. He also must retain his objectivity and not allow his feelings and emotions or a rush to judgment to color his work. If the latter should take place, justice is not served and an innocent person may be subjected to unnecessary humiliation. An example of this occurred when Mr. Jewell was publicly identified as the primary suspect in the Olympic Games bombing incident in Atlanta, GA, in 1997. It was later proved that he had nothing to do with the bombing. Another person was responsible for this incident and several other bombings that resulted in the deaths of a number of innocent people.

The Collection and Use of Samples and Specimens

A sample is defined as being "a small part of or a selection from something, intended to show the quality, style, or nature of the whole."[17] A specimen is defined as: "1. a part or an individual taken as exemplifying a whole mass or number, such as a typical animal, mineral, etc.; 2. a sample of a substance or material for examination or study; 3. a particular or peculiar kind of person."[17] In an investigation, how samples and specimens are collected is determined by what is needed for comparison purposes. The procedures for obtaining them are well established and must be followed, if sufficient evidence for comparison purposes is to be obtained. If not, the collection process is for naught.

The sample may be of a person's handwriting, typed material prepared on a specific typewriter, etc. A specimen may consist of blood, seminal fluids, hair, fibers and threads, paint, tool marks, inked prints, etc. Regardless of whether it is a sample or specimen, what is obtained is determined by the type of case being investigated, what is found at the crime scene, and what is needed for comparison purposes by the laboratory. Many books and papers have been written on how to collect evidence, samples, and specimens. Most of the older books and papers do not take into account the requirements set forth for laboratory accreditation by the American Society of Crime Laboratory Directors (ASCLAD). ASCLAD has adopted four objectives to define the purposes and nature of the program:[18]

1. To improve the quality of laboratory services provided to the criminal justice system
2. To develop and maintain criteria which can be used by a laboratory to assess its level of performance and to strengthen it operation
3. To provide an independent, impartial, and objective system by which laboratories can benefit from a total operational review
4. To offer to the general public and to users of laboratory services a means of identifying those laboratories which have demonstrated that they meet established standards

ASCLAD requirements reach out of the laboratory to the crime scene and the investigator. Following are general procedures that could be used by a law enforcement agency seeking to ensure evidence integrity:[18]

1. The collection of all evidence at a crime scene will be in accordance with accepted and recognized procedures to ensure that the evidence is not contaminated.
2. All evidence is properly marked for identification at the crime scene.
3. All evidence is described completely and properly documented so there is no mistake about what was collected and where it was found.
4. A complete and accurate documented chain of custody of all evidence is maintained.

5. All evidence is properly package for shipment to and from the laboratory; there must never be any chance of damage to evidence during shipment.
6. All evidence is securely sealed in individual packages so any tampering attempt is detectable and to ensure that no evidence is lost.
7. A secure location for evidence is established within the receiving office and limited access is granted during storage and examination.

The next section of this chapter describes how a case should be submitted to the Questioned Document Laboratory by an investigator. Several examples are given to illustrate what has been discussed here concerning the collection and use of evidence in a questioned document case.

How Should the Investigator Submit a Case to the Questioned Document Laboratory?

A case involving questioned documents (i.e., credit cards, counterfeit checks, or IDs) is given to the investigator for investigation in a manner similar to our story and the situation presented in the story at the beginning of this section. When the investigator receives the evidence, he may find, for example, that it contains two suspect counterfeit credit cards, five suspect counterfeit checks, and a checkbook and register with six missing checks and six entries in the register. There are also these items: a suspected counterfeit ID card and a suspected genuine ID card with the same name but not the picture of the victim. The suspected counterfeit ID contains the picture of a person currently held in detention. What does the investigator do now?

He performs a preliminary inspection of the evidence. This preliminary inspection is done while the investigator wears gloves so as not to contaminate the evidence. He should make several copies of each document in question — one copy for his work file to write notes on, a copy for the office file, and one to submit with the original evidence when it goes to the laboratory. Other copies may be necessary as circumstances warrant. Each copy, though, should be made from the original evidence and not from a previously made copy.

For illustration purposes, the following assumptions are made:

1. The suspected counterfeit cards, IDs, and payer signatures on the checks repeat the same name: John R. Smith.[19]
2. The IDs are driver's licenses suspected of being issued by the same state.
3. The checkbook contains six missing checks that must be located; there are entries for the six missing checks written on the check register.
4. The investigator has all of the questioned documents, except the checks.

First, the investigator contacts the companies and individuals to whom the missing checks are written and the bank on which they are drawn. His purpose, if possible, is to obtain the original checks. After obtaining them, he places them in sealed transparent evidence envelopes that are properly marked in accordance with accepted evidence handling procedures.

Next, he prepares to interview several suspects and obtain handwriting samples and fingerprints. Proper and adequate handwriting samples and clearly recorded inked prints are critical to the examination and results reached by the laboratory. The general guidelines for obtaining sample writing are

1. Know what writing is in question. Have the suspect repeat it and nonrepetitive material numerous times. *The investigator must never allow the suspect to see the questioned material at any time.* The questioned material should be dictated to the suspect, or typed on a sheet of paper that is provided to the suspect during the session. The investigator should also obtain some nonrepetitive material such as that found on a standard handwriting sample form, such as the alphabet, random names, addresses, numbers, etc.
2. Watch the suspect as he writes the samples. All too frequently, a suspect will try to disguise his specimen writing. To determine whether he is attempting to do so, the investigator should have a sample of the suspect's normal handwriting. The investigator can get a copy of his driver's license from the DMV and perhaps other business writings before the interview and writing session. He may even ask the suspect to identify himself by producing identification documents prior to the interview; the investigator should then make several copies of these samples for his file and for comparison purposes.
3. Remove completed specimens from the suspect's view so he cannot use them as a reference of how he just wrote certain features. The main idea here is to get as much writing as possible, representing the normal variation found in the suspect's writing, for comparison purposes. If the suspect can see what he has written and how he shaped the previously written letters, it is easier for him to be consistent is his attempt to disguise his writing.
4. Note any instructions given to the suspect on the sample writing sheet where the instruction is given. All instructions should be noted on the handwriting form, initialed by both the investigator and suspect so there is no confusion about what the suspect was asked to do.

There is more to taking handwriting samples than is given here. The above is just a brief summary of some of the more important aspects of this part of the investigator's work. The rolling of inked prints has not been discussed here. There are numerous books written on the subject that should be referred to by the reader, because their authors are more qualified than this writer to explain the techniques and intricacies of rolling inked prints for comparison purposes.

After collecting evidence at the crime scene and obtaining the handwriting samples, how should the investigator submit all of these items to the laboratory and what should he ask the laboratory to do? He should:

1. Follow the general guidelines given above for collecting evidence at the crime scene and taking handwriting specimens from a suspect.

2. Prepare a comprehensive work request using the following example as a model.

Questioned Document Work Request

Submitted Exhibits

1. Q-1. One First National Bank Visa credit card embossed with account no. 4234 5678 9012 3456 and the name John R. Smith, initialed and dated RNM/3/3/98 and identified with the number Q-1.
2. Q-2. One First National Bank MasterCard credit card embossed with account no. 5123 4567 8901 2345 and the name John R. Smith, initialed and dated RNM/3/3/98 and identified with the number Q-2.
3. Q-3 through Q-8. Six checks drawn on First National Bank, respectively numbered 100 through 105, signed John R. Smith, payer, initialed and dated RNM/3/3/98 and identified with the numbers Q-3 through Q-7 respectively.
4. Q-9 through Q-14. One checkbook with register having six missing checks with preprinted numbers and six entries dated 2/12/97 in the register next to the numbers 100 through 105. The book and register are initialed and dated RNM/3/3/98. Each individual entry is assigned a "Q" number as follows: check no. 100, Q-8; check no. 101, Q-9; etc.
5. Q-15. One driver's license no. 123456 in the name of John R. Smith, initialed and dated RNM/3/3/98 and identified with the number Q-15.
6. Q-16. One driver's license no. 123456 in the name of John R. Smith, initialed and dated RNM/3/3/98 and identified with the number Q-16.
7. S-1. Twenty-five specimen handwriting forms numbered 1 through 25, signed John R. Smith, witnessed by HKD, and dated 3/9/98.

The initials and date referred to on each item should be those of the investigator when he inventoried the evidence at the crime scene or interviewed the suspect and obtained the handwriting samples. The examiner must also initial and date each item when he conducts his examination in the laboratory. Documents Q-15 and Q-16 both contain the same identifying information but have different people shown in the photograph on each card. One of the documents, let us say Q-15, belonged to the victim in this case. The next part of the work request should specify just what examinations the investigator wants done with the evidence.

Examinations Desired

1. Determine whether Exhibits Q-1, Q-2, Q-15, and Q-16 are counterfeit.
2. Determine whether Exhibits Q-1 and Q-2 were embossed on the same embossing machine.
3. Determine whether the magnetic stripes on Exhibits Q-1 and Q-2 are encoded, what information is encoded on each stripe, and whether they were encoded on the same or similar encoders.

4. Determine whether the author of the specimen writing described as S-1 wrote the questioned signatures on Exhibits Q-1 and Q-2, all of the handwriting on the face and endorsement on the back of Exhibits Q-3 through Q-8, the six entries on the register (Exhibits Q-9 through Q-14), and the signatures on Q-15 and Q-16.

What critical information remains for the examiner to know? When does the investigator need the results and a written report? Such information should go in a "Remarks" section of the work request. The Questioned Document Examiner receiving this case will need about one week to conduct the examinations described above, evaluate his findings, meet ASCLAD requirements, and report the results of his work to the investigator.

What Results Should the Investigator Expect?

He should expect a clearly written report from the examiner describing the items examined, the examinations conducted on each item, and the result of each examination. A sample work request is described above. The basic elements of that document should also appear in the report. Next is a discussion of the examiner's report to the investigator and return of the evidence to him.

Elements of a Forensic Report

At the conclusion of an examination, the examiner must produce a clearly written report that describes:

1. Documents examined
2. Examinations requested
3. Results of the examinations
4. Disposition of the submitted documents
5. Other relevant remarks

The outline of the report in some ways mirrors the format of the work request submitted by the investigator. If the submitted items are described accurately on the work request, the examiner can use the same number designation and description of each item in his report. If he does this, there is less confusion between the investigator and him concerning the submitted items.

As with all of his cases, the examiner uses language to inform the recipient of the report about the results of his examinations. Because language is not always precise, the same words can have different, or slightly different, actual or semantical meanings to the reader. Some examiners use a number of qualifying words and phrases in the same sentence. For example, it is *possible* that the writer of the S-1 specimens could have written the questioned signature. Which is it ... he *probably* wrote it or he *could have* written it? The words or phrases chosen may not convey a clear understanding of the degree of belief the examiner reached as a result of his work. Other examiners use brief statements with few qualifying words and phrases. To assist the recipient of a handwriting/hand-printing report in understanding the language used and concepts behind the language, the writer may attach a brief description of the language and its meaning in the report.

The following examples represent brief and clearly written statements used to express the degree of belief the examiner has based upon the result of his examination:

1. "It has been concluded that John Doe wrote..."
2. "It has been concluded that John Doe in all probability wrote..." (at times, the phrase "in all probability wrote" may be substituted with "very probably wrote" or "it is highly probable that John Doe wrote")
3. "It has been concluded that John Doe probably wrote..."
4. "There is some evidence to suggest, or to indicate, that John Doe wrote..."
5. "It could not be determined whether John Doe wrote the questioned material."
6. "With the material available for comparison, no evidence was found to suggest that John Doe wrote..."
7. "There is some evidence to suggest, or to indicate, that John Doe did not write..."
8. "It has been concluded that John Doe probably did not write..."
9. "It has been concluded that in all probability John Doe did not write..." (the same terms "very probably" or "it is highly probable" may also be used to replace "in all probability")
10. "It has been concluded that John Doe did not write..."

Defining Terms

What do these statements mean? How should the reader interpret or understand them in the context of a report? The first statement is unequivocal. It has been said, "There is no stronger opinion given by a document examiner in a handwriting case than a positive identification."[20] When he uses this statement, the examiner has no reservation whatsoever about the certainty of his conclusion. He is so certain of his conclusion that for him it is a fact that the writer of the samples and questioned material are the same person. Because he can only express an opinion in a court of law, he is prohibited from testifying that it is a fact that the questioned and sample writings are by the same writer. What is the standard for such a strong belief? Briefly stated, there must be complete agreement in all features of writing important for identification purposes with no significant differences or dissimilarities that would suggest another writer is involved. Also, the writing must contain both class and individual features which, when taken collectively, are in excellent agreement with no significant or fundamental differences or dissimilarities in writing habits. However, there are occasions when a difference or dissimilarity is observed, but its presence is far outweighed by agreement in the significant features and must be concluded to be the result of a variation in the writer's writing.

The second statement is used when the evidence falls just short of the requirement for an identification. At times, the phrase "in all probability" may be substituted with "very probably wrote" or "it is highly probable that John Doe wrote." Regardless of the words used, the examiner has some slight reservation or reason for not making a categorical statement. Maybe there is the absence of one or even two features having some significance. He may have a question about the quality of the writing which he believes is important for identification and cannot be resolved with the available writing. Regardless of the reason, he selects his language carefully, because it reflects his belief based on his examination of the available evidence.

The third statement is used when the evidence points rather strongly toward the writer of the sample, but still falls short of the requirements for the prior qualified opinion. Even though there are significant similarities present between the questioned and sample writing, there are also irreconcilable differences that cannot be explained with the available writing. These irreconcilable differences may have varying degrees of significance. For example, if the questioned or sample writing is a photocopy and the examiner is not able to determine stroke direction or line quality characteristics sufficiently, he might choose to express his degree of belief by using this statement. If this statement is too strong, he may use some other more qualified language to express his degree of belief. By way of example, the importance of determining stroke direction or line quality for every feature may be outweighed by the collective significance of other qualities and features present in the writing that are equally, or more, important for identification purposes. Therefore, the examiner may then choose to use this language. While there is, by definition, a greater likelihood of someone else writing the questioned material than is expressed in the previous opinion (the second statement), the evidence is still pointing rather strongly in the direction of the specimen writer. Most people believe that when the word "probable" is used, it means a 50% chance of some event occurring. That meaning does not apply here. When the examiner uses this qualifier, he is saying that there is more evidence to suggest the writer of the sample wrote the questioned material than there is to suggest he did not write the questioned material. Probable has been defined as "...having more evidence for than against, or evidence that inclines the mind to belief but leaves some room for doubt."[21]

The fourth statement is used when there are a few handwriting features in agreement and some may have more significance for identification than others. The examiner is saying to the reader of the report, "Keep this writer in mind." Although there is not a sufficient amount of evidence to say that the writer of the sample probably wrote the questioned material, there are some writing features in agreement which suggest he has the skill and ability to write it. However, the significance of those features that do agree is limited.

The fifth statement is used when the examiner is not able to determine whether the specimen writer wrote the questioned material. Before he begins his examination, the examiner does not know whether or not the writers of the samples wrote the questioned material. His position as an examiner must be neutral. The purpose of his examination is to try to determine whether the writers wrote the questioned material. There are many occasions when the examiner is not able to proceed any further than when he began his examination. This usually occurs when there is no significant evidence for or against identifying the writer of the samples as the writer of the questioned documents.

The same general principles apply to the degrees of belief expressing negative opinions. In many cases, the evidence present varies in significance. It must be added that an elimination opinion is harder to reach than an identification opinion. There are technical reasons for this statement that go beyond the scope of this work and therefore will not be covered here.

Regardless of the type of written report, it must clearly and accurately describe the evidence examined, the work requested, the results of that work, and what disposition was made of the evidence submitted for examination. The results of the examination must be clearly written so the work that was done and the results of that work are easily understood by the reader. The use of clearly written phrases, concepts, and language is an essential element of a report. The disposition of evidence should be in accordance with standard procedures. By writing all reports following these principles, the examiner is better able to communicate with the investigator, officer of the court, judge, and the jury should he have to testify.

Summary

The use of Forensic Scientists and their disciplines by the investigator can greatly assist him in his investigation. The Forensic Scientist should be brought in at the beginning of the case, as in our story, not just before the case goes to trial. Too often investigators wait until the last minute to submit evidence to the laboratory for analysis. In those situations, it is frequently necessary to continue the trial because the forensic examinations are not complete or the results of those examinations have produced new information that must be checked out by the investigator before the trial begins.

The investigator spends a lot of time conducting his investigation. The evidence he develops during the coarse of that investigation can yield significant information that may not otherwise be available. The evidence at the crime scene helps to tell the story of what events took place there at a particular moment in time. It has a story of its own to tell that may or may not be consistent with the statements of witnesses. The importance of "interviewing" this evidence by careful examination in the laboratory cannot be overstated. Our story is typical of many financial crimes involving counterfeit documents, but, in this case, because the investigator and examiners worked together from the beginning, the chances of a successful prosecution of the guilty parties were greatly increased.

Notes

1. Newton, J., *Organised "Plastic" Counterfeiting,* Crown Publishers, London, 1994.
2. *The New Britannica/Webster Dictionary & Reference Guide,* Encyclopedia Britannica, Chicago, 1986.

3. *Webster's Electronic Dictionary & Thesaurus,* College Edition, Random House, San Francisco, CA, 1992.
4. O'Hara, C.E. and Osterburg, J.W., *An Introduction to Criminalistics: The Application of the Physical Sciences to the Detection of Crime,* Indiana University Press, Bloomington, 1972, p. 3.
5. This material on crime scenes was drawn from *Crime Scene Response Guidelines III: Organization and Procedures for Search Operations,* at http://www.police2.ucr.edu/respon3.html.
6. Hilton, O., *Scientific Examination of Questioned Documents,* rev. ed., Elsevier-North Holland, New York, 1982, p. 4; Osborn, A.S., A new profession, *Journal of American Judicature Society,* 24, 1940 (reprinted in Osborn, A.S. and Osborn, A.D., *Questioned Document Problems,* 2nd ed., Boyd, Albany, NY, 1946, pp. 358–367).
7. Hilton, O., *Scientific Examination of Questioned Documents,* rev. ed., Elsevier-North Holland, New York, 1982, p. 5.
8. Cole, A., *Studies in Document Analysis,* June 10, 1959. Cole was the Examiner of Questioned Documents for the U.S. Treasury Department, in Washington, D.C., prior to his retirement and later passing. The referenced paper is one of many he wrote during a very long and distinguished career.
9. Morris, R.N., Embosser type: a three-dimensional type examination, *The International Journal of Forensic Document Examiners,* 4(2), 1998.
10. Harrison, W.R., *Suspect Documents: Their Scientific Examination,* Sweet & Maxwell, London, 1966, p. 288.
11. Cantu, A.A., verbal communication, July 24, 1998.
12. FBI Fingerprint Identification website, http://www.fbi.gov/kids/finger/finger.html.
13. Figure 3 was provided by the FBI, Fugitive Publicity Internet Media Services Unit. It is a more up-to-date version of the one referred to in Note 12, above. The authors are indebted to the FBI for their contribution.
14. *Webster's Electronic Dictionary & Thesaurus,* College Edition, Random House, San Francisco, CA, 1992.
15. van Renesse, R.L., Ed., *Optical Document Security,* Artech House, Boston, MA, 1994, p. 25.
16. van Renesse, R.L., Ed., *Optical Document Security,* Artech House, Boston, MA, 1994, p. 28.
17. *Webster's Electronic Dictionary & Thesaurus,* College Edition, Random House, San Francisco, CA, 1992.
18. Morris, R.N., Evidence, *International Review of Law Computers & Technology,* 12(2), 309, 1998.
19. Any relationship between this name and an actual person is coincidental. The name used here was chosen only for illustration purposes.
20. Over the years, Thomas V. McAlexander has written several papers and articles on this topic. This information is based, in part, on his and other examiners' work trying to establish a common language for questioned document and handwriting reports.
21. *Webster's Electronic Dictionary & Thesaurus,* College Edition, Random House, San Francisco, CA, 1992.

Appendixes

Appendix A. Fraud and the U.S. Federal Code

The following sections includes various titles and relative sections for the U.S. Federal Code.

18 USC Section 1028 01/26/98

–EXPCITE–

TITLE 18 — CRIMES AND CRIMINAL PROCEDURE

PART I — CRIMES

CHAPTER 47 — FRAUD AND FALSE STATEMENTS

–HEAD–

Sec. 1028. Fraud and related activity in connection with identification documents

–STATUTE–

(a) Whoever, in a circumstance described in subsection (c) of this section —

(1) knowingly and without lawful authority produces an identification document or a false identification document;

(2) knowingly transfers an identification document or a false identification document knowing that such document was stolen or produced without lawful authority;

(3) knowingly possesses with intent to use unlawfully or transfer unlawfully five or more identification documents (other than those issued lawfully for the use of the possessor) or false identification documents;

(4) knowingly possesses an identification document (other than one issued lawfully for the use of the possessor) or a false identification document, with the intent such document be used to defraud the United States;

(5) knowingly produces, transfers, or possesses a document-making implement with the intent such document-making implement will be used in the production of a false identification document or another document-making implement which will be so used; or

(6) knowingly possesses an identification document that is or appears to be an identification document of the United States which is stolen or produced without lawful authority knowing that such document was stolen or produced without such authority; or attempts to do so, shall be punished as provided in subsection (b) of this section.

(b) The punishment for an offense under subsection (a) of this section is —

(1) except as provided in paragraphs (3) and (4), a fine under this title or imprisonment for not more than 15 years, or both, if the offense is —

(A) the production or transfer of an identification document or false identification document that is or appears to be —

(i) an identification document issued by or under the authority of the United States; or

(ii) a birth certificate, or a driver's license or personal identification card;

(B) the production or transfer of more than five identification documents or false identification documents; or

(C) an offense under paragraph (5) of such subsection;

(2) except as provided in paragraphs (3) and (4), a fine under this title or imprisonment for not more than three years, or both, if the offense is —

(A) any other production or transfer of an identification document or false identification document; or

(B) an offense under paragraph (3) of such subsection;

(3) a fine under this title or imprisonment for not more than 20 years, or both, if the offense is committed to facilitate a drug trafficking crime (as defined in section 929(a)(2) of this title);

(4) a fine under this title or imprisonment for not more than 25 years, or both, if the offense is committed to facilitate an act of international terrorism (as defined in section 2331(1) of this title); and

(5) a fine under this title or imprisonment for not more than one year, or both, in any other case.

(c) The circumstance referred to in subsection (a) of this section is that —

(1) the identification document or false identification document is or appears to be issued by or under the authority of the United States or the document-making implement is designed or suited for making such an identification document or false identification document;

(2) the offense is an offense under subsection (a)(4) of this section; or

(3) the production, transfer, or possession prohibited by this section is in or affects interstate or foreign commerce, or the identification document, false identification document, or document-making implement is transported in the mail in the course of the production, transfer, or possession prohibited by this section.

(d) As used in this section —

(1) the term "identification document" means a document made or issued by or under the authority of the United States Government, a State, political subdivision of a State, a foreign government, political subdivision of a foreign government, an international governmental or an international quasi-governmental organization which, when completed with information concerning a particular individual, is of a type intended or commonly accepted for the purpose of identification of individuals;

(2) the term "produce" includes alter, authenticate, or assemble;

(3) the term "document-making implement" means any implement or impression specially designed or primarily used for making an identification document, a false identification document, or another document-making implement;

(4) the term "personal identification card" means an identification document issued by a State or local government solely for the purpose of identification; and

(5) the term "State" includes any State of the United States, the District of Columbia, the Commonwealth of Puerto Rico, and any other commonwealth, possession or territory of the United States.

(e) This section does not prohibit any lawfully authorized investigative, protective, or intelligence activity of a law enforcement agency of the United States, a State, or a political subdivision of a State, or of an intelligence agency of the United States, or any activity authorized under chapter 224 of this title.

–SOURCE–

(Added Pub. L. 97-398, Sec. 2, Dec. 31, 1982, 96 Stat. 2009; amended Pub. L. 99-646, Sec. 44(a), Nov. 10, 1986, 100 Stat. 3601; Pub. L. 100-690, title VII, Sec. 7023, Nov. 18, 1988,

102 Stat. 4397; Pub. L. 101-647, title XII, Sec. 1205(e), Nov. 29, 1990, 104 Stat. 4831; Pub. L. 103-322, title XXXIII, Sec. 330016(1)(K), (M), (O), Sept. 13, 1994, 108 Stat. 2147, 2148; Pub. L. 104-208, div. C, title II, Sec. 211(a)(1), Sept. 30, 1996, 110 Stat. 3009-569; Pub. L. 104-294, title VI, Sec. 601(a)(3), (p), Oct. 11, 1996, 110 Stat. 3498, 3502.)

–MISC1–

AMENDMENTS

1996 – Subsec. (a)(4), (5). Pub. L. 104-294, Sec. 601(p), struck out "or" after semicolon in par. (4) and inserted "or" after semicolon in par. (5).

Subsec. (b). Pub. L. 104-294, Sec. 601(a)(3), substituted "fine under this title" for "fine of under this title" wherever appearing.

Subsec. (b)(1). Pub. L. 104-208, Sec. 211(a)(1)(A), in introductory provisions inserted "except as provided in paragraphs (3) and (4)," after "(1)" and substituted "15 years" for "five years".

Subsec. (b)(2). Pub. L. 104-208, Sec. 211(a)(1)(B), inserted "except as provided in paragraphs (3) and (4)," after "(2)" in introductory provisions and struck out "and" at end.

Subsec. (b)(3) to (5). Pub. L. 104-208, Sec. 211(a)(1)(C), (D), added pars. (3) and (4) and redesignated former par. (3) as (5).

1994 – Subsec. (b)(1). Pub. L. 103-322, Sec. 330016(1)(O), substituted "under this title" for "not more than $25,000".

Subsec. (b)(2). Pub. L. 103-322, Sec. 330016(1)(M), substituted "under this title" for "not more than $15,000".

Subsec. (b)(3). Pub. L. 103-322, Sec. 330016(1)(K), substituted "under this title" for "not more than $5,000".

1990 – Subsec. (d)(5). Pub. L. 101-647 inserted "commonwealth," before "possession or territory of the United States".

1988 – Subsec. (a)(6). Pub. L. 100-690 inserted "knowingly" before "possesses", "lawful" before first reference to "authority", and "such" before second reference to "authority".

1986 – Subsec. (e). Pub. L. 99-646 substituted "chapter 224 of this title" for "title V of the Organized Crime Control Act of 1970 (18 USC note prec. 3481)".

EFFECTIVE DATE OF 1996 AMENDMENT

Section 211(c) of div. C of Pub. L. 104-208 provided that: "This section (amending this section and sections 1425 to 1427, 1541 to 1544, and 1546 of this title and enacting provisions set out as a note under section 994 of Title 28, Judiciary and Judicial Procedure) and the amendments made by this section shall apply with respect to offenses occurring on or after the date of the enactment of this Act (Sept. 30, 1996)."

FRAUD AND RELATED ACTIVITY IN CONNECTION WITH IDENTIFICATION DOCUMENTS

Pub. L. 98-473, title II, Sec. 609L, Oct. 12, 1984, 98 Stat. 2103, provided that:

"(a) For purposes of section 1028 of title 18, United States Code, to the maximum extent feasible, personal descriptors or identifiers utilized in identification documents, as defined in such section, shall utilize common descriptive terms and formats designed to —

> "(1) reduce the redundancy and duplication of identification systems by providing information which can be utilized by the maximum number of authorities, and
>
> "(2) facilitate positive identification of bona fide holders of identification documents.

"(b) The President shall, no later than 3 years after the date of enactment of this Act (Oct. 12, 1984), and after consultation with Federal, State, local, and international issuing authorities, and concerned groups make recommendations (recommendations) to the Congress for the enactment of comprehensive legislation on Federal identification systems. Such legislation shall —

> "(1) give due consideration to protecting the privacy of persons who are the subject of any identification system,
>
> "(2) recommend appropriate civil and criminal sanctions for the misuse or unauthorized disclosure of personal identification information, and
>
> "(3) make recommendations providing for the exchange of personal identification information as authorized by Federal or State law or Executive order of the President or the chief executive officer of any of the several States."

–SECREF–

SECTION REFERRED TO IN OTHER SECTIONS

This section is referred to in sections 922, 981, 982, 2257, 2326, 2516 of this title; title 8 section 1324a; title 22 section 2709; title 31 section 9703; title 42 section 5119a.

18 USC Section 1029

–EXPCITE–

TITLE 18 – CRIMES AND CRIMINAL PROCEDURE

PART I – CRIMES

CHAPTER 47 – FRAUD AND FALSE STATEMENTS

–HEAD–

Sec. 1029. Fraud and related activity in connection with access devices

–STATUTE–

(a) Whoever —

(1) knowingly and with intent to defraud produces, uses, or traffics in one or more counterfeit *access devices*;

(2) knowingly and with intent to defraud traffics in or uses one or more unauthorized *access devices* during any one-year period, and by such conduct obtains anything of value aggregating $1000 or more during that period;

(3) knowingly and with intent to defraud possesses fifteen or more *devices* which are counterfeit or unauthorized *access devices*;

(4) knowingly, and with intent to defraud, produces, traffics in, has control or custody of, or possesses *device*-making equipment;

(5) knowingly and with intent to defraud effects transactions, with 1 or more *access devices* issued to another person or persons, to receive payment or any other thing of value during any 1-year period the aggregate value of which is equal to or greater than $1,000;

(6) without the authorization of the issuer of the *access device*, knowingly and with intent to defraud solicits a person for the purpose of —

(A) offering an *access device*; or

(B) selling information regarding or an application to obtain an *access device*;

(7) knowingly and with intent to defraud uses, produces, traffics in, has control or custody of, or possesses a telecommunications instrument that has been modified or altered to obtain unauthorized use of telecommunications services;

(8) knowingly and with intent to defraud uses, produces, traffics in, has control or custody of, or possesses —

(A) a scanning receiver; or

(B) hardware or software used for altering or modifying telecommunications instruments to obtain unauthorized *access* to telecommunications services, (FOOTNOTE 1)

(FOOTNOTE 1) So in original. The comma probably should be a semicolon.

(9) without the authorization of the credit card system member or its agent, knowingly and with intent to defraud causes or arranges for another person to present to the member or its agent, for payment, 1 or more evidences or records of transactions made by an *access device*; shall, if the offense affects interstate or foreign commerce, be punished as provided in subsection (c) of this section.

(b) (1) Whoever attempts to commit an offense under subsection (a) of this section shall be punished as provided in subsection (c) of this section.

(2) Whoever is a party to a conspiracy of two or more persons to commit an offense under subsection (a) of this section, if any of the parties engages in any conduct in furtherance of such offense, shall be fined an amount not greater than the amount provided as the maximum fine for such offense under subsection (c) of this section or imprisoned not longer than one-half the period provided as the maximum imprisonment for such offense under subsection (c) of this section, or both.

(c) The punishment for an offense under subsection (a) or (b)(1) of this section is —

(1) a fine under this title or twice the value obtained by the offense, whichever is greater, or imprisonment for not more than ten years, or both, in the case of an offense under subsection (a)(2), (3), (5), (6), (7), (8), or (9) of this section which does not occur after a conviction for another offense under either such subsection, or an attempt to commit an offense punishable under this paragraph;

(2) a fine under this title or twice the value obtained by the offense, whichever is greater, or imprisonment for not more than fifteen years, or both, in the case of an offense under subsection (a)(1), (4), (5), (6), (7), or (8) of this section which does not occur after a conviction for another offense under either such subsection, or an attempt to commit an offense punishable under this paragraph; and

(3) a fine under this title or twice the value obtained by the offense, whichever is greater, or imprisonment for not more than twenty years, or both, in the case of an offense under subsection (a) of this section which occurs after a conviction for another offense under such subsection, or an attempt to commit an offense punishable under this paragraph.

(d) The United States Secret Service shall, in addition to any other agency having such authority, have the authority to investigate offenses under this section. Such authority of the United States Secret Service shall be exercised in accordance with an agreement which shall be entered into by the Secretary of the Treasury and the Attorney General.

(e) As used in this section —

(1) the term "*access device*" means any card, plate, code, account number, electronic serial number, mobile identification number, personal identification number, or other telecommunications service, equipment, or instrument identifier, or other means of account *access* that can be used, alone or in conjunction with another *access device*, to obtain money, goods, services, or any other thing of value, or that can be used to initiate a transfer of funds (other than a transfer originated solely by paper instrument);

(2) the term "counterfeit *access device*" means any *access device* that is counterfeit, fictitious, altered, or forged, or an identifiable component of an *access device* or a counterfeit *access device*;

(3) the term "unauthorized *access device*" means any *access device* that is lost, stolen, expired, revoked, canceled, or obtained with intent to defraud;

(4) the term "produce" includes design, alter, authenticate, duplicate, or assemble;

(5) the term "traffic" means transfer, or otherwise dispose of, to another, or obtain control of with intent to transfer or dispose of;

(6) the term "*device*-making equipment" means any equipment, mechanism, or impression designed or primarily used for making an *access device* or a counterfeit *access device*; and

(7) the term "credit card system member" means a financial institution or other entity that is a member of a credit card system, including an entity, whether affiliated with or identical to the credit card issuer, that is the sole member of a credit card system.

(8) the term "scanning receiver" means a *device* or apparatus that can be used to intercept a wire or electronic communication in violation of chapter 119.

(f) This section does not prohibit any lawfully authorized investigative, protective, or intelligence activity of a law enforcement agency of the United States, a State, or a political subdivision of a State, or of an intelligence agency of the United States, or any activity authorized under chapter 224 of this title. For purposes of this subsection, the term "State" includes a State of the United States, the District of Columbia, and any commonwealth, territory, or possession of the United States.

–SOURCE–

(Added Pub. L. 98-473, title II, Sec. 1602(a), Oct. 12, 1984, 98 Stat. 2183; amended Pub. L. 99-646, Sec. 44(b), Nov. 10, 1986, 100 Stat. 3601; Pub. L. 101-647, title XII, Sec. 1205(f), Nov. 29, 1990, 104 Stat. 4831; Pub. L. 103-322, title XXV, Sec. 250007, title XXXIII, Sec. 330016(2)(I), Sept. 13, 1994, 108 Stat. 2087, 2148; Pub. L. 103-414, title II, Sec. 206, Oct. 25, 1994, 108 Stat. 4291; Pub. L. 104-294, title VI, Sec. 601(l), Oct. 11, 1996, 110 Stat. 3501.)

–MISC1–

AMENDMENTS

1996 – Subsec. (a)(5). Pub. L. 104-294, Sec. 601(l)(1)(A), redesignated par. (5), relating to instruments that have been modified or altered to obtain unauthorized *access* to telecommunications services, as (7).

Subsec. (a)(6). Pub. L. 104-294, Sec. 601(l)(1)(C), in par. (6) relating to solicitations, struck out "or" at end.

Pub. L. 104-294, Sec. 601(l)(1)(A), redesignated par. (6), relating to scanning receivers or other hardware or software used to obtain unauthorized *access* to telecommunications services, as (8).

Subsec. (a)(7). Pub. L. 104-294, Sec. 601(l)(1)(A), (C), redesignated par. (5), relating to instruments that have been modified or altered to obtain unauthorized *access* to telecommunications services, as (7), and struck out "or" at end.

Par. transferred to appear in numerical order to reflect probable intent of Congress. Former par. (7) redesignated (9).

Pub. L. 104-294, Sec. 601(l)(1)(B), redesignated par. (7) as (9).

Subsec. (a)(8). Pub. L. 104-294, Sec. 601(l)(1)(A), (D), redesignated par. (6), relating to scanning receivers or other hardware or software used to obtain unauthorized *access* to telecommunications services, as (8) and inserted "or" at end.

Par. transferred to appear in numerical order to reflect probable intent of Congress.

Subsec. (a)(9). Pub. L. 104-294, Sec. 601(l)(1)(B), redesignated par. (7) as (9).

Subsec. (c)(1). Pub. L. 104-294, Sec. 601(l)(3)(A), substituted "(7), (8), or (9)" for "or (7)".

Subsec. (c)(2). Pub. L. 104-294, Sec. 601(l)(3)(B), substituted "(6), (7), or (8)" for "or (6)".

Subsec. (e)(7), (8). Pub. L. 104-294, Sec. 601(l)(2), redesignated par. (7), defining "scanning receiver", as (8).

1994 – Subsec. (a)(3). Pub. L. 103-322, Sec. 250007(1)(A), and Pub. L. 103-414, Sec. 206(a)(1), amended par. (3) identically, striking "or" at end.

Subsec. (a)(5). Pub. L. 103-414, Sec. 206(a)(2), added par. (5) relating to instruments that have been modified or altered to obtain unauthorized use of telecommunications services.

Pub. L. 103-322, Sec. 250007(1)(B), added par. (5) relating to transactions involving use of *access devices* issued to persons other than user.

Subsec. (a)(6). Pub. L. 103-414, Sec. 206(a)(2), added par. (6) relating to scanning receivers or other hardware or software used to obtain unauthorized *access* to telecommunications services.

Pub. L. 103-322, Sec. 250007(1)(B), added par. (6) relating to solicitations which offer *access devices* or information regarding *access devices.*

Subsec. (a)(7). Pub. L. 103-322, Sec. 250007(1)(B), added par. (7).

Subsec. (c)(1). Pub. L. 103-322, Sec. 330016(2)(I), substituted "fine under this title or twice the value obtained by the offense, whichever is greater, or imprisonment" for "fine of not more than the greater of $10,000 or twice the value obtained by the offense or imprisonment".

Pub. L. 103-322, Sec. 250007(2), substituted "(a)(2), (3), (5), (6), or (7)" for "(a)(2) or (a)(3)".

Subsec. (c)(2). Pub. L. 103-414, Sec. 206(b), substituted "(a)(1), (4), (5), or (6)" for "(a)(1) or (a)(4)".

Pub. L. 103-322, Sec. 330016(2)(I), substituted "fine under this title or twice the value obtained by the offense, whichever is greater, or imprisonment" for "fine of not more than the greater of $50,000 or twice the value obtained by the offense or imprisonment".

Subsec. (c)(3). Pub. L. 103-322, Sec. 330016(2)(I), substituted "fine under this title or twice the value obtained by the offense, whichever is greater, or imprisonment" for "fine of not more than the greater of $100,000 or twice the value obtained by the offense or imprisonment".

Subsec. (e)(1). Pub. L. 103-414, Sec. 206(c)(1), inserted "electronic serial number, mobile identification number, personal identification number, or other telecommunications service, equipment, or instrument identifier," after "account number,".

Subsec. (e)(5), (6). Pub. L. 103-322, Sec. 250007(3)(A), (B), and Pub. L. 103-414, Sec. 206(c)(2), (3), amended subsec. (e) identically, striking "and" at end of par. (5) and substituting "; and" for period at end of par. (6).

Subsec. (e)(7). Pub. L. 103-414, Sec. 206(c)(4), added par. (7) defining "scanning receiver".

Pub. L. 103-322, Sec. 250007(3)(C), added par. (7) defining "credit card system member".

1990 - Subsec. (f). Pub. L. 101-647 inserted at end "For purposes of this subsection, the term 'State' includes a State of the United States, the District of Columbia, and any commonwealth, territory, or possession of the United States."

1986 – Subsec. (f). Pub. L. 99-646 which directed that subsec. (f) be amended by substituting "chapter 224 of this title" for "title V of the Organized Crime Control Act of 1970 (18 USC note prec. 3481)" was executed by making the substitution for "title V of the Organized Crime Control Act of 1970) 18 USC note prec. 3481)" to reflect the probable intent of Congress.

REPORT TO CONGRESS

Section 1603 of Pub. L. 98-473 directed Attorney General to report to Congress annually, during first three years following Oct. 12, 1984, concerning prosecutions under this section.

–SECREF–

SECTION REFERRED TO IN OTHER SECTIONS

This section is referred to in sections 981, 982, 1030, 1961, 2326, 2516 of this title; title 31 section 9703.

18 USC Section 1030

–EXPCITE–

TITLE 18 — CRIMES AND CRIMINAL PROCEDURE

PART I — CRIMES

CHAPTER 47 — FRAUD AND FALSE STATEMENTS

–HEAD–

Sec. 1030. Fraud and related activity in connection with computers

–STATUTE–

(a) Whoever —

(1) having knowingly *accessed* a computer without authorization or exceeding authorized *access*, and by means of such conduct having obtained information that has been determined by the United States Government pursuant to an Executive order or statute to require protection against unauthorized disclosure for reasons of national defense or foreign relations, or any restricted data, as defined in paragraph y. of section 11 of the Atomic Energy Act of 1954, with reason to believe that such information so obtained could be used to the injury of the United States, or to the advantage of any foreign nation willfully communicates, delivers, transmits, or causes to be communicated, delivered, or transmitted, or attempts to communicate, deliver, transmit or cause to be communicated, delivered, or transmitted the same to any person not entitled to receive it, or willfully retains the same and fails to deliver it to the officer or employee of the United States entitled to receive it;

(2) intentionally *accesses* a computer without authorization or exceeds authorized *access*, and thereby obtains —

(A) information contained in a financial record of a financial institution, or of a card issuer as defined in section 1602(n) of title 15, or contained in a file of a consumer reporting agency on a consumer, as such terms are defined in the Fair Credit Reporting Act (15 USC 1681 et seq.);

(B) information from any department or agency of the United States; or

(C) information from any protected computer if the conduct involved an interstate or foreign communication;

(3) intentionally, without authorization to *access* any nonpublic computer of a department or agency of the United States, *accesses* such a computer of that department or agency that is exclusively for the use of the Government of the United States or, in the case of a computer not exclusively for such use, is used by or for the Government of the United States and such conduct affects that use by or for the Government of the United States;

(4) knowingly and with intent to defraud, *accesses* a protected computer without authorization, or exceeds authorized *access*, and by means of such conduct furthers the intended fraud and obtains anything of value, unless the object of the fraud and the thing obtained consists only of the use of the computer and the value of such use is not more than $5,000 in any 1-year period;

(5) (A) knowingly causes the transmission of a program, information, code, or command, and as a result of such conduct, intentionally causes damage without authorization, to a protected computer;

(B) intentionally *accesses* a protected computer without authorization, and as a result of such conduct, recklessly causes damage; or

(C) intentionally *accesses* a protected computer without authorization, and as a result of such conduct, causes damage;

(6) knowingly and with intent to defraud traffics (as defined in section 1029) in any password or similar information through which a computer may be *accessed* without authorization, if —

(A) such trafficking affects interstate or foreign commerce; or

(B) such computer is used by or for the Government of the United States; (FOOTNOTE 1)

(FOOTNOTE 1) So in original. Probably should be followed by "or".

(7) with intent to extort from any person, firm, association, educational institution, financial institution, government entity, or other legal entity, any money or other thing of value, transmits in interstate or foreign commerce any communication containing any threat to cause damage to a protected computer; shall be punished as provided in subsection (c) of this section.

(b) Whoever attempts to commit an offense under subsection (a) of this section shall be punished as provided in subsection (c) of this section.

(c) The punishment for an offense under subsection (a) or (b) of this section is —

(1) (A) a fine under this title or imprisonment for not more than ten years, or both, in the case of an offense under subsection (a)(1) of this section which does not occur after a conviction for another offense under this section, or an attempt to commit an offense punishable under this subparagraph; and

(B) a fine under this title or imprisonment for not more than twenty years, or both, in the case of an offense under subsection (a)(1) of this section which occurs after a conviction for another offense under this section, or an attempt to commit an offense punishable under this subparagraph;

(2) (A) a fine under this title or imprisonment for not more than one year, or both, in the case of an offense under subsection (a)(2), (a)(3), (a)(5)(C), or (a)(6) of this section which does not occur after a conviction for another of-

fense under this section, or an attempt to commit an offense punishable under this subparagraph; (FOOTNOTE 2)

(FOOTNOTE 2) So in original. The word "and" probably should not appear.

(B) a fine under this title or imprisonment for not more than 5 years, or both, in the case of an offense under subsection (a)(2), if —

(i) the offense was committed for purposes of commercial advantage or private financial gain;

(ii) the offense was committed in furtherance of any criminal or tortuous act in violation of the Constitution or laws of the United States or of any State; or

(iii) the value of the information obtained exceeds $5000; (FOOTNOTE 3)

(FOOTNOTE 3) So in original. Probably should be followed by "and".

(C) a fine under this title or imprisonment for not more than ten years, or both, in the case of an offense under subsection (a)(2), (a)(3) or (a)(6) of this section which occurs after a conviction for another offense under this section, or an attempt to commit an offense punishable under this subparagraph; and

(3) (A) a fine under this title or imprisonment for not more than five years, or both, in the case of an offense under subsection (a)(4), (a)(5)(A), (a)(5)(B), or (a)(7) of this section which does not occur after a conviction for another offense under this section, or an attempt to commit an offense punishable under this subparagraph; and

(B) a fine under this title or imprisonment for not more than ten years, or both, in the case of an offense under subsection (a)(4), (a)(5)(A), (a)(5)(B), (a)(5)(C), or (a)(7) of this section which occurs after a conviction for another offense under this section, or an attempt to commit an offense punishable under this subparagraph; and (FOOTNOTE 4)

(FOOTNOTE 4) So in original. The "; and" probably should be a period.

(d) The United States Secret Service shall, in addition to any other agency having such authority, have the authority to investigate offenses under subsections (a)(2)(A), (a)(2)(B), (a)(3), (a)(4), (a)(5), and (a)(6) of this section. Such authority of the United States Secret Service shall be exercised in accordance with an agreement which shall be entered into by the Secretary of the Treasury and the Attorney General.

(e) As used in this section —

(1) the term "computer" means an electronic, magnetic, optical, electrochemical, or other high speed data processing device performing logical, arithmetic, or storage functions, and includes any data storage facility or communications

facility directly related to or operating in conjunction with such device, but such term does not include an automated typewriter or typesetter, a portable hand held calculator, or other similar device;

(2) the term "protected computer" means a computer —

(A) exclusively for the use of a financial institution or the United States Government, or, in the case of a computer not exclusively for such use, used by or for a financial institution or the United States Government and the conduct constituting the offense affects that use by or for the financial institution or the Government; or

(B) which is used in interstate or foreign commerce or communication;

(3) the term "State" includes the District of Columbia, the Commonwealth of Puerto Rico, and any other commonwealth, possession or territory of the United States;

(4) the term "financial institution" means —

(A) an institution, with deposits insured by the Federal Deposit Insurance Corporation;

(B) the Federal Reserve or a member of the Federal Reserve including any Federal Reserve Bank;

(C) a credit union with accounts insured by the National Credit Union Administration;

(D) a member of the Federal home loan bank system and any home loan bank;

(E) any institution of the Farm Credit System under the Farm Credit Act of 1971;

(F) a broker-dealer registered with the Securities and Exchange Commission pursuant to section 15 of the Securities Exchange Act of 1934;

(G) the Securities Investor Protection Corporation;

(H) a branch or agency of a foreign bank (as such terms are defined in paragraphs (1) and (3) of section 1(b) of the International Banking Act of 1978); and

(I) an organization operating under section 25 or section 25(a) (FOOTNOTE 5) of the Federal Reserve Act. (FOOTNOTE 6)

(FOOTNOTE 5) See References in text note below.

(FOOTNOTE 6) So in original. The period probably should be a semicolon.

(5) the term "financial record" means information derived from any record held by a financial institution pertaining to a customer's relationship with the financial institution;

(6) the term "exceeds authorized *access*" means to *access* a computer with authorization and to use such *access* to obtain or alter information in the computer that the *accesser* is not entitled so to obtain or alter;

(7) the term "department of the United States" means the legislative or judicial branch of the Government or one of the executive departments enumerated in section 101 of title 5; and (FOOTNOTE 7)

(FOOTNOTE 7) So in original. The word "and" probably should not appear.

(8) the term "damage" means any impairment to the integrity or availability of data, a program, a system, or information, that —

(A) causes loss aggregating at least $5,000 in value during any 1-year period to one or more individuals;

(B) modifies or impairs, or potentially modifies or impairs, the medical examination, diagnosis, treatment, or care of one or more individuals;

(C) causes physical injury to any person; or

(D) threatens public health or safety; and

(9) the term "government entity" includes the Government of the United States, any State or political subdivision of the United States, any foreign country, and any state, province, municipality, or other political subdivision of a foreign country.

(f) This section does not prohibit any lawfully authorized investigative, protective, or intelligence activity of a law enforcement agency of the United States, a State, or a political subdivision of a State, or of an intelligence agency of the United States.

(g) Any person who suffers damage or loss by reason of a violation of this section may maintain a civil action against the violator to obtain compensatory damages and injunctive relief or other equitable relief. Damages for violations involving damage as defined in subsection (e)(8)(A) are limited to economic damages. No action may be brought under this subsection unless such action is begun within 2 years of the date of the act complained of or the date of the discovery of the damage.

(h) The Attorney General and the Secretary of the Treasury shall report to the Congress annually, during the first 3 years following the date of the enactment of this subsection, concerning investigations and prosecutions under subsection (a)(5).

–SOURCE–

(Added Pub. L. 98-473, title II, Sec. 2102(a), Oct. 12, 1984, 98 Stat. 2190; amended Pub. L. 99-474, Sec. 2, Oct. 16, 1986, 100 Stat. 1213; Pub. L. 100-690, title VII, Sec. 7065, Nov. 18, 1988, 102 Stat. 4404; Pub. L. 101-73, title IX, Sec. 962(a)(5), Aug. 9, 1989, 103 Stat. 502; Pub. L. 101-647, title XII, Sec. 1205(e), title XXV, Sec. 2597(j), title XXXV, Sec. 3533, Nov. 29, 1990, 104 Stat. 4831, 4910, 4925; Pub. L. 103-322, title XXIX, Sec. 290001(b)-(f), Sept. 13, 1994, 108 Stat. 2097-2099; Pub. L. 104-294, title II, Sec. 201, title VI, Sec. 604(b)(36), Oct. 11, 1996, 110 Stat. 3491, 3508.)

REFERENCES IN TEXT

Section 11 of the Atomic Energy Act of 1954, referred to in subsec. (a)(1), is classified to section 2014 of Title 42, The Public Health and Welfare. The Fair Credit Reporting Act, referred to in subsec. (a)(2)(A), is title VI of Pub. L. 90-321, as added by Pub. L. 91-508, title VI, Sec. 601, Oct. 26, 1970, 84 Stat. 1127, as amended, which is classified generally to subchapter III (Sec. 1681 et seq.) of chapter 41 of Title 15, Commerce and Trade. For complete classification of this Act to the Code, see Short Title note set out under section 1601 of Title 15 and Tables. The Farm Credit Act of 1971, referred to in subsec. (e)(4)(E), is Pub. L. 92-181, Dec. 10, 1971, 85 Stat. 583, as amended, which is classified generally to chapter 23 (Sec. 2001 et seq.) of Title 12, Banks and Banking. For complete classification of this Act to the Code, see Short Title note set out under section 2001 of Title 12 and Tables. Section 15 of the Securities Exchange Act of 1934, referred to in subsec. (e)(4)(F), is classified to section 78o of Title 15, Commerce and Trade. Section 1(b) of the International Banking Act of 1978, referred to in subsec. (e)(4)(H), is classified to section 3101 of Title 12, Banks and Banking. Section 25 of the Federal Reserve Act, referred to in subsec. (e)(4)(I), is classified to subchapter I (Sec. 601 et seq.) of chapter 6 of Title 12. Section 25(a) of the Federal Reserve Act, which is classified to subchapter II (Sec. 611 et seq.) of chapter 6 of Title 12, was renumbered section 25A of that act by Pub. L. 102-242, title I, Sec. 142(e)(2), Dec. 19, 1991, 105 Stat. 2281. The date of the enactment of this subsection, referred to in subsec. (h), is the date of enactment of Pub. L. 103-322, which was approved Sept. 13, 1994.

–MISC1–

AMENDMENTS

1996 – Subsec. (a)(1). Pub. L. 104-294, Sec. 201(1)(A), substituted "having knowingly *accessed*" for "knowingly *accesses*", "exceeding authorized *access*" for "exceeds authorized *access*", "such conduct having obtained information" for "such conduct obtains information", and "could be used to the injury of the United States" for "is to be used to the injury of the United States", struck out "the intent or" before "reason to believe", and inserted before semicolon at end "willfully communicates, delivers, transmits, or causes to be communicated, delivered, or transmitted, or attempts to communicate, deliver, transmit or cause to be communicated, delivered, or transmitted the same to any person not entitled to receive it, or willfully retains the same and fails to deliver it to the officer or employee of the United States entitled to receive it".

Subsec. (a)(2). Pub. L. 104-294, Sec. 201(1)(B), inserted dash after "thereby obtains", redesignated remainder of par. (2) as subpar. (A), and added subpars. (B) and (C).

Subsec. (a)(3). Pub. L. 104-294, Sec. 201(1)(C), inserted "nonpublic" before "computer of a department or agency", struck out "adversely" after "and such conduct", and substituted "that use by or for the Government of the United States" for "the use of the Government's operation of such computer".

Subsec. (a)(4). Pub. L. 104-294, Sec. 201(1)(D), substituted "protected computer" for "Federal interest computer" and inserted "and the value of such use is not more than $5000 in any 1-year period" before semicolon at end.

Subsec. (a)(5). Pub. L. 104-294, Sec. 201(1)(E), inserted par. (5) and struck out former par. (5) which related to fraud in connection with computers in causing transmission of program, information, code, or command to a computer or computer system in interstate or foreign commerce which damages such system, program, information, or code, or causes a withholding or denial of use of hardware or software, or transmits viruses which causes damage in excess of $1,000 or more during any one-year period, or modifies or impairs medical examination, diagnosis, treatment or care of individuals.

Subsec. (a)(5)(B)(ii)(II)(bb). Pub. L. 104-294, Sec. 604(b)(36)(A), which directed insertion of "or" at end of subsec., could not be executed because no subsec. (a)(5)(B)(ii)(II)(bb) existed subsequent to amendment by Pub. L. 104-294, Sec. 201(1)(E). See above.

Subsec. (a)(7). Pub. L. 104-294, Sec. 201(1)(F), added par. (7).

Subsec. (c)(1). Pub. L. 104-294, Sec. 201(2)(A), substituted "under this section" for "under such subsection" in subpars. (A) and (B).

Subsec. (c)(1)(B). Pub. L. 104-294, Sec. 604(b)(36)(B), struck out "and" after semicolon at end.

Subsec. (c)(2)(A). Pub. L. 104-294, Sec. 201(2)(B)(i), inserted ", (a)(5)(C)," after "(a)(3)" and substituted "under this section" for "under such subsection".

Subsec. (c)(2)(B). Pub. L. 104-294, Sec. 201(2)(B)(iii), added subpar. (B). Former subpar. (B) redesignated (C).

Subsec. (c)(2)(C). Pub. L. 104-294, Sec. 201(2)(B)(iv), substituted "under this section" for "under such subsection" and inserted "and" at end. Pub. L. 104-294, Sec. 201(2)(B)(ii), redesignated subpar. (B) as (C).

Subsec. (c)(3)(A). Pub. L. 104-294, Sec. 201(2)(C)(i), substituted "(a)(4), (a)(5)(A), (a)(5)(B), or (a)(7)" for "(a)(4) or (a)(5)(A)" and "under this section" for "under such subsection".

Subsec. (c)(3)(B). Pub. L. 104-294, Sec. 201(2)(C)(ii), substituted "(a)(4), (a)(5)(A), (a)(5)(B), (a)(5)(C), or (a)(7)" for "(a)(4) or (a)(5)" and "under this section" for "under such subsection". Subsec. (c)(4). Pub. L. 104-294, Sec. 201(2)(D), struck out par. (4) which read as follows: "a fine under this title or imprisonment for not more than 1 year, or both, in the case of an offense under subsection (a)(5)(B)."

Subsec. (d). Pub. L. 104-294, Sec. 201(3), inserted "subsections (a)(2)(A), (a)(2)(B), (a)(3), (a)(4), (a)(5), and (a)(6) of" before "this section" in first sentence. Subsec. (e)(2). Pub. L. 104-294, Sec. 201(4)(A)(i), substituted "protected" for "Federal interest" in introductory provisions.

Subsec. (e)(2)(A). Pub. L. 104-294, Sec. 201(4)(A)(ii), substituted "that use by or for the financial institution or the Government" for "the use of the financial institution's operation or the Government's operation of such computer".

Subsec. (e)(2)(B). Pub. L. 104-294, Sec. 201(4)(A)(iii), added subpar. (B) and struck out former subpar. (B) which read as follows: "which is one of two or more computers used in committing the offense, not all of which are located in the same State;".

Subsec. (e)(8), (9). Pub. L. 104-294, Sec. 201(4)(B)-(D), added pars. (8) and (9).

Subsec. (g). Pub. L. 104-294, Sec. 604(b)(36)(C), substituted "violation of this section" for "violation of the section".

Pub. L. 104-294, Sec. 201(5), struck out ", other than a violation of subsection (a)(5)(B)," before "may maintain a civil action" and substituted "involving damage as defined in subsection (e)(8)(A)" for "of any subsection other than subsection (a)(5)(A)(ii)(II)(bb) or (a)(5)(B)(ii)(II)(bb)".

Subsec. (h). Pub. L. 104-294, Sec. 604(b)(36)(D), substituted "subsection (a)(5)" for "section 1030(a)(5) of title 18, United States Code" before period at end.

1994 – Subsec. (a)(3). Pub. L. 103-322, Sec. 290001(f), inserted "adversely" before "affects the use of the Government's".

Subsec. (a)(5). Pub. L. 103-322, Sec. 290001(b), amended par. (5) generally. Prior to amendment, par. (5) read as follows: "intentionally *accesses* a Federal interest computer without authorization, and by means of one or more instances of such conduct alters, damages, or destroys information in any such Federal interest computer, or prevents authorized use of any such computer or information, and thereby —

> "(A) causes loss to one or more others of a value aggregating $1000 or more during any one year period; or
>
> "(B) modifies or impairs, or potentially modifies or impairs, the medical examination, medical diagnosis, medical treatment, or medical care of one or more individuals; or".

Subsec. (c)(3)(A). Pub. L. 103-322, Sec. 290001(c)(2), inserted "(A)" after "(a)(5)".

Subsec. (c)(4). Pub. L. 103-322, Sec. 290001(c)(1), (3), (4), added par. (4).

Subsec. (g). Pub. L. 103-322, Sec. 290001(d), added subsec. (g).

Subsec. (h). Pub. L. 103-322, Sec. 290001(e), added subsec. (h).

1990 – Subsec. (a)(1). Pub. L. 101-647, Sec. 3533, substituted "paragraph y" for "paragraph r".

Subsec. (e)(3). Pub. L. 101-647, Sec. 1205(e), inserted "commonwealth," before "possession or territory of the United States".

Subsec. (e)(4)(G). Pub. L. 101-647, Sec. 2597(j)(2), which directed substitution of a semicolon for a period at end of subpar. (G), could not be executed because it ended with a semicolon.

Subsec. (e)(4)(H), (I). Pub. L. 101-647, Sec. 2597(j), added subpars. (H) and (I).

1989 – Subsec. (e)(4)(A). Pub. L. 101-73, Sec. 962(a)(5)(A), substituted "an institution," for "a bank".

Subsec. (e)(4)(C) to (H). Pub. L. 101-73, Sec. 962(a)(5)(B), (C), redesignated subpars. (D) to (H) as (C) to (G), respectively, and struck out former subpar. (C) which read as follows: "an institution with accounts insured by the Federal Savings and Loan Insurance Corporation;".

1988 – Subsec. (a)(2). Pub. L. 100-690 inserted a comma after "financial institution" and struck out the comma that followed a comma after "title 15".

1986 – Subsec. (a). Pub. L. 99-474, Sec. 2(b)(2), struck out last sentence which read as follows: "It is not an offense under paragraph (2) or (3) of this subsection in the case of a person having *accessed* a computer with authorization and using the opportunity such *access* provides for purposes to which such *access* does not extend, if the using of such opportunity consists only of the use of the computer."

Subsec. (a)(1). Pub. L. 99-474, Sec. 2(c), substituted "or exceeds authorized *access*" for ", or having *accessed* a computer with authorization, uses the opportunity such *access* provides for purposes to which such authorization does not extend".

Subsec. (a)(2). Pub. L. 99-474, Sec. 2(a), (c), substituted "intentionally" for "knowingly", substituted "or exceeds authorized *access*" for ", or having *accessed* a computer with authorization, uses the opportunity such *access* provides for purposes to which such authorization does not extend", struck out "as such terms are defined in the Right to Financial Privacy Act of 1978 (12 USC 3401 et seq.)," after "financial institution,", inserted "or of a card issuer as defined in section 1602(n) of title 15," and struck out "or" appearing at end.

Subsec. (a)(3). Pub. L. 99-474, Sec. 2(b)(1), amended par. (3) generally. Prior to amendment, par. (3) read as follows: "knowingly *accesses* a computer without authorization, or having *accessed* a computer with authorization, uses the opportunity such *access* provides for purposes to which such authorization does not extend, and by means of such conduct knowingly uses, modifies, destroys, or discloses information in, or prevents authorized use of, such computer, if such computer is operated for or on behalf of the Government of the United States and such conduct affects such operation;".

Subsec. (a)(4) to (6). Pub. L. 99-474, Sec. 2(d), added pars. (4) to (6).

Subsec. (b). Pub. L. 99-474, Sec. 2(e), struck out par. (1) designation and par. (2) which provided a penalty for persons conspiring to commit an offense under subsec. (a).

Subsec. (c). Pub. L. 99-474, Sec. 2(f)(9), substituted "(b)" for "(b)(1)" in introductory text.

Subsec. (c)(1)(A). Pub. L. 99-474, Sec. 2(f)(1), substituted "under this title" for "of not more than the greater of $10,000 or twice the value obtained by the offense".

Subsec. (c)(1)(B). Pub. L. 99-474, Sec. 2(f)(2), substituted "under this title" for "of not more than the greater of $100,000 or twice the value obtained by the offense".

Subsec. (c)(2)(A). Pub. L. 99-474, Sec. 2(f)(3), (4), substituted "under this title" for "of not more than the greater of $5,000 or twice the value obtained or loss created by the offense" and inserted reference to subsec. (a)(6).

Subsec. (c)(2)(B). Pub. L. 99-474, Sec. 2(f)(3), (5)-(7), substituted "under this title" for "of not more than the greater of $10,000 or twice the value obtained or loss created by the offense", "not more than" for "not than", inserted reference to subsec. (a)(6), and substituted "; and" for the period at end of subpar. (B).

Subsec. (c)(3). Pub. L. 99-474, Sec. 2(f)(8), added par. (3).

Subsec. (e). Pub. L. 99-474, Sec. 2(g), substituted a dash for the comma after "As used in this section", realigned remaining portion of subsection, inserted "(1)" before "the term", substituted a semicolon for the period at the end, and added pars. (2) to (7).

Subsec. (f). Pub. L. 99-474, Sec. 2(h), added subsec. (f).

REPORTS TO CONGRESS

Section 2103 of Pub. L. 98-473 directed Attorney General to report to Congress annually, during first three years following Oct. 12, 1984, concerning prosecutions under this section.

–SECREF–

SECTION REFERRED TO IN OTHER SECTIONS

This section is referred to in sections 981, 982, 2256, 3239 of this title; title 31 section 9703.

18 USC Section 1031

–EXPCITE–

TITLE 18 — CRIMES AND CRIMINAL PROCEDURE

PART I — CRIMES

CHAPTER 47 — FRAUD AND FALSE STATEMENTS

–HEAD–

Sec. 1031. Major fraud against the United States

–STATUTE–

(a) Whoever knowingly executes, or attempts to execute, any scheme or artifice with the intent —

(1) to defraud the United States; or

(2) to obtain money or property by means of false or fraudulent pretenses, representations, or promises, in any procurement of property or services as a prime contractor with the United States or as a subcontractor or supplier on a contract in which there is a prime contract with the United States, if the value of the contract, subcontract, or any constituent part thereof, for such property or services is $1,000,000 or more shall, subject to the applicability of subsection (c) of this section, be fined not more than $1,000,000, or imprisoned not more than 10 years, or both.

(b) The fine imposed for an offense under this section may exceed the maximum otherwise provided by law, if such fine does not exceed $5,000,000 and —

(1) the gross loss to the Government or the gross gain to a defendant is $500,000 or greater; or

(2) the offense involves a conscious or reckless risk of serious personal injury.

(c) The maximum fine imposed upon a defendant for a prosecution including a prosecution with multiple counts under this section shall not exceed $10,000,000.

(d) Nothing in this section shall preclude a court from imposing any other sentences available under this title, including without limitation a fine up to twice the amount of the gross loss or gross gain involved in the offense pursuant to 18 USC section 3571(d).

(e) In determining the amount of the fine, the court shall consider the factors set forth in 18 USC sections 3553 and 3572, and the factors set forth in the guidelines and policy statements of the United States Sentencing Commission, including —

(1) the need to reflect the seriousness of the offense, including the harm or loss to the victim and the gain to the defendant;

(2) whether the defendant previously has been fined for a similar offense; and

(3) any other pertinent equitable considerations.

(f) A prosecution of an offense under this section may be commenced any time not later than 7 years after the offense is committed, plus any additional time otherwise allowed by law.

(g) (1) In special circumstances and in his or her sole discretion, the Attorney General is authorized to make payments from funds appropriated to the Department of Justice to persons who furnish information relating to a possible prosecution under this section. The amount of such payment shall not exceed

$250,000. Upon application by the Attorney General, the court may order that the Department shall be reimbursed for a payment from a criminal fine imposed under this section.

(2) An individual is not eligible for such a payment if —

(A) that individual is an officer or employee of a Government agency who furnishes information or renders service in the performance of official duties;

(B) that individual failed to furnish the information to the individual's employer prior to furnishing it to law enforcement authorities, unless the court determines the individual has justifiable reasons for that failure;

(C) the furnished information is based upon public disclosure of allegations or transactions in a criminal, civil, or administrative hearing, in a congressional, administrative, or GAO report, hearing, audit or investigation, or from the news media unless the person is the original source of the information. For the purposes of this subsection, "original source" means an individual who has direct and independent knowledge of the information on which the allegations are based and has voluntarily provided the information to the Government; or

(D) that individual participated in the violation of this section with respect to which such payment would be made.

(3) The failure of the Attorney General to authorize a payment shall not be subject to judicial review.

(h) Any individual who —

(1) is discharged, demoted, suspended, threatened, harassed, or in any other manner discriminated against in the terms and conditions of employment by an employer because of lawful acts done by the employee on behalf of the employee or others in furtherance of a prosecution under this section (including investigation for, initiation of, testimony for, or assistance in such prosecution), and

(2) was not a participant in the unlawful activity that is the subject of said prosecution, may, in a civil action, obtain all relief necessary to make such individual whole. Such relief shall include reinstatement with the same seniority status such individual would have had but for the discrimination, 2 times the amount of back pay, interest on the back pay, and compensation for any special damages sustained as a result of the discrimination, including litigation costs and reasonable attorney's fees.

–SOURCE–

(Added Pub. L. 100-700, Sec. 2(a), Nov. 19, 1988, 102 Stat. 4631; amended Pub. L. 101-123, Sec. 2(a), Oct. 23, 1989, 103 Stat. 759; Pub. L. 103-322, title XXXIII, Sec. 330002(a), (f), Sept. 13, 1994, 108 Stat. 2140.)

–MISC1–

AMENDMENTS

1994 – Subsec. (g). Pub. L. 103-322, Sec. 330002(f), redesignated second subsec. (g) as (h).

Subsec. (g)(2)(A). Pub. L. 103-322, Sec. 330002(a), substituted "a Government" for "a government".

Subsec. (h). Pub. L. 103-322, Sec. 330002(f), redesignated second subsec. (g) as (h).

1989 – Subsec. (g). Pub. L. 101-123 added, after subsec. (f), subsec. (g) relating to payments by the Attorney General.

EFFECTIVE DATE OF 1989 AMENDMENT

Section 2(b) of Pub. L. 101-123 provided that: "The amendment made by this section (amending this section) shall apply to contracts entered into on or after the date of the enactment of this Act (Oct. 23, 1989)."

SENTENCING GUIDELINES

Section 2(b) of Pub. L. 100-700 provided that: "Pursuant to its authority under section 994(p) of title 28, United States Code and section 21 of the Sentencing Act of 1987 (section 21 of Pub. L. 100-182, set out as a note under section 994 of Title 28, Judiciary and Judicial Procedure), the United States Sentencing Commission shall promulgate guidelines, or shall amend existing guidelines, to provide for appropriate penalty enhancements, where conscious or reckless risk of serious personal injury resulting from the fraud has occurred. The Commission shall consider the appropriateness of assigning to such a defendant an offense level under Chapter Two of the sentencing guidelines that is at least two levels greater than the level that would have been assigned had conscious or reckless risk of serious personal injury not resulted from the fraud."

–SECREF–

SECTION REFERRED TO IN OTHER SECTIONS

This section is referred to in sections 981, 982 of this title.

18 USC Section 1341

–EXPCITE–

TITLE 18 — CRIMES AND CRIMINAL PROCEDURE

PART I — CRIMES

CHAPTER 63 — MAIL FRAUD

–HEAD–

Sec. 1341. Frauds and swindles

–STATUTE–

Whoever, having devised or intending to devise any scheme or artifice to defraud, or for obtaining money or property by means of false or fraudulent pretenses, representations, or promises, or to sell, dispose of, loan, exchange, alter, give away, distribute, supply, or furnish or procure for unlawful use any counterfeit or spurious coin, obligation, security, or other article, or anything represented to be or intimated or held out to be such counterfeit or spurious article, for the purpose of executing such scheme or artifice or attempting so to do, places in any post office or authorized depository for mail matter, any matter or thing whatever to be sent or delivered by the Postal Service, or deposits or causes to be deposited any matter or thing whatever to be sent or delivered by any private or commercial interstate carrier, or takes or receives therefrom, any such matter or thing, or knowingly causes to be delivered by mail or such carrier according to the direction thereon, or at the place at which it is directed to be delivered by the person to whom it is addressed, any such matter or thing, shall be fined under this title or imprisoned not more than five years, or both. If the violation affects a financial institution, such person shall be fined not more than $1,000,000 or imprisoned not more than 30 years, or both.

–SOURCE–

(June 25, 1948, ch. 645, 62 Stat. 763; May 24, 1949, ch. 139, Sec. 34, 63 Stat. 94; Aug. 12, 1970, Pub. L. 91-375, Sec. (6)(j)(11), 84 Stat. 778; Aug. 9, 1989, Pub. L. 101-73, title IX, Sec. 961(i), 103 Stat. 500; Nov. 29, 1990, Pub. L. 101-647, title XXV, Sec. 2504(h), 104 Stat. 4861; Sept. 13, 1994, Pub. L. 103-322, title XXV, Sec. 250006, title XXXIII, Sec. 330016(1)(H), 108 Stat. 2087, 2147.)

HISTORICAL AND REVISION NOTES

1948 ACT

Based on title 18, USC, 1940 ed., Sec. 338 (Mar. 4, 1909, ch. 321, Sec. 215, 35 Stat. 1130).

The obsolete argot of the underworld was deleted as suggested by Hon. Emerich B. Freed, United States district judge, in a paper read before the 1944 Judicial Conference for the sixth circuit in which he said:

A brief reference to Sec. 1341, which proposes to reenact the present section covering the use of the mails to defraud. This section is almost a page in length, is involved, and contains a great deal of superfluous language, including such terms as "sawdust swindle, green articles, green coin, green goods and green cigars." This section could be greatly simplified, and now-meaningless language eliminated.

The other surplusage was likewise eliminated and the section simplified without change of meaning. A reference to causing to be placed any letter, etc. in any post office, or station thereof, etc. was omitted as unnecessary because of definition of "principal" in section 2 of this title.

1949 ACT

This section (section 34) corrects a typographical error in section 1341 of title 18, USC.

–MISC1–

AMENDMENTS

1994 – Pub. L. 103-322, Sec. 330016(1)(H), substituted "fined under this title" for "fined not more than $1000" after "thing, shall be". Pub. L. 103-322, Sec. 250006, inserted "or deposits or causes to be deposited any matter or thing whatever to be sent or delivered by any private or commercial interstate carrier," after "Postal Service," and "or such carrier" after "causes to be delivered by mail".

1990 – Pub. L. 101-647 substituted "30" for "20" before "years".

1989 – Pub. L. 101-73 inserted at end "If the violation affects a financial institution, such person shall be fined not more than $1,000,000 or imprisoned not more than 20 years, or both."

1970 – Pub. L. 91-375 substituted "Postal Service" for "Post Office Department".

1949 – Act May 24, 1949, substituted "of" for "or" after "dispose".

EFFECTIVE DATE OF 1970 AMENDMENT

Amendment by Pub. L. 91-375 effective within 1 year after Aug. 12, 1970, on date established therefor by Board of Governors of United States Postal Service and published by it in Federal Register, see section 15(a) of Pub. L. 91-375, set out as an Effective Date note preceding section 101 of Title 39, Postal Service.

CROSS REFERENCES

Fictitious name or address used in frauds and swindles, see section 1342 of this title.

Postal Service, offenses against, see section 1691 et seq. of this title.

Seizure and disposition of nonmailable matter, see section 3001 of Title 39, Postal Service.

Use of fictitious, false or assumed name on mail to conduct, or assist in, activity in violation of this section, see section 3003 of Title 39.

Use of mails for purchase or sale of securities before a registration statement under "Securities Act, 1933" is in effect made unlawful, see section 77e of Title 15, Commerce and Trade.

–SECREF–

SECTION REFERRED TO IN OTHER SECTIONS

This section is referred to in sections 24, 225, 981, 982, 1342, 1510, 1961, 2326, 2516, 3059A, 3293, 3322 of this title; title 7 section 12a; title 12 sections 1785, 1786, 1787, 1821, 1828, 1829, 1831k, 1833a, 2277a-10b; title 15 sections 78o, 80b-3; title 39 sections 3001, 3003.

18 USC Section 1342

–EXPCITE–

TITLE 18 — CRIMES AND CRIMINAL PROCEDURE

PART I — CRIMES

CHAPTER 63 — MAIL FRAUD

–HEAD–

Sec. 1342. Fictitious name or address

–STATUTE–

Whoever, for the purpose of conducting, promoting, or carrying on by means of the Postal Service, any scheme or device mentioned in section 1341 of this title or any other unlawful business, uses or assumes, or requests to be addressed by, any fictitious, false, or assumed title, name, or address or name other than his own proper name, or takes or receives from any post office or authorized depository of mail matter, any letter, postal card, package, or other mail matter addressed to any such fictitious, false, or assumed title, name, or address, or name other than his own proper name, shall be fined under this title or imprisoned not more than five years, or both.

–SOURCE–

(June 25, 1948, ch. 645, 62 Stat. 763; Aug. 12, 1970, Pub. L. 91-375, Sec. 6(j)(12), 84 Stat. 778; Sept. 13, 1994, Pub. L. 103-322, title XXXIII, Sec. 330016(1)(H), 108 Stat. 2147.)

HISTORICAL AND REVISION NOTES

Based on title 18, USC, 1940 ed., Sec. 339 (Mar. 4, 1909, ch. 321, Sec. 216, 35 Stat. 1131). The punishment language used in section 1341 of this title was substituted in lieu of the reference to it in this section. Minor changes in phraseology were made.

–MISC1–

AMENDMENTS

1994 – Pub. L. 103-322 substituted "fined under this title" for "fined not more than $1000".

1970 – Pub. L. 91-375 substituted "Postal Service" for "Post Office Department of the United States".

EFFECTIVE DATE OF 1970 AMENDMENT

Amendment by Pub. L. 91-375 effective within 1 year after Aug. 12, 1970, on date established therefor by Board of Governors of United States Postal Service and published by it in Federal Register, see section 15(a) of Pub. L. 91-375, set out as an Effective Date note preceding section 101 of Title 39, Postal Service.

CROSS REFERENCES

Seizure and disposition of nonmailable matter, see section 3001 of Title 39, Postal Service. Use of fictitious, false or assumed name on mail to conduct, or assist in, activity in violation of this section, see section 3003 of Title 39.

–SECREF–

SECTION REFERRED TO IN OTHER SECTIONS

This section is referred to in section 2326 of this title; title 7 section 12a; title 15 sections 78o, 80b-3; title 39 sections 3001, 3003.

18 USC Section 1343

–EXPCITE–

TITLE 18 — CRIMES AND CRIMINAL PROCEDURE

PART I — CRIMES

CHAPTER 63 — MAIL FRAUD

–HEAD–

Sec. 1343. Fraud by wire, radio, or television

–STATUTE–

Whoever, having devised or intending to devise any scheme or artifice to defraud, or for obtaining money or property by means of false or fraudulent pretenses, representations, or promises, transmits or causes to be transmitted by means of wire, radio, or television communication in interstate or foreign commerce, any writings, signs, signals, pictures, or sounds for the purpose of executing such scheme or artifice, shall be fined under this title or imprisoned not more than five years, or both. If the violation affects a financial institution, such person shall be fined not more than $1,000,000 or imprisoned not more than 30 years, or both.

–SOURCE–

(Added July 16, 1952, ch. 879, Sec. 18(a), 66 Stat. 722; amended July 11, 1956, ch. 561, 70 Stat. 523; Aug. 9, 1989, Pub. L. 101-73, title IX, Sec. 961(j), 103 Stat. 500; Nov. 29, 1990, Pub. L. 101-647, title XXV, Sec. 2504(i), 104 Stat. 4861; Sept. 13, 1994, Pub. L. 103-322, title XXXIII, Sec. 330016(1)(H), 108 Stat. 2147.)

–MISC1–

AMENDMENTS

1994 – Pub. L. 103-322 substituted "fined under this title" for "fined not more than $1000".

1990 – Pub. L. 101-647 substituted "30" for "20" before "years".

1989 – Pub. L. 101-73 inserted at end "If the violation affects a financial institution, such person shall be fined not more than $1,000,000 or imprisoned not more than 20 years, or both."

1956 – Act July 11, 1956, substituted "transmitted by means of wire, radio, or television communication in interstate or foreign commerce" for "transmitted by means of interstate wire, radio, or television communication".

–SECREF–

SECTION REFERRED TO IN OTHER SECTIONS

This section is referred to in sections 24, 225, 981, 982, 1510, 1961, 2326, 2516, 3059A, 3293, 3322 of this title; title 7 section 12a; title 12 sections 1785, 1786, 1787, 1821, 1828, 1829, 1831k, 1833a, 2277a-10b; title 15 sections 78o, 80b-3; title 47 sections 312, 503.

18 USC Section 1344

–EXPCITE–

TITLE 18 — CRIMES AND CRIMINAL PROCEDURE

PART I — CRIMES

CHAPTER 63 — MAIL FRAUD

–HEAD–

Sec. 1344. Bank fraud

–STATUTE–

Whoever knowingly executes, or attempts to execute, a scheme or artifice —

(1) to defraud a financial institution; or

(2) to obtain any of the moneys, funds, credits, assets, securities, or other property owned by, or under the custody or control of, a financial institution, by means of false or fraudulent pretenses, representations, or promises; shall be fined not more than $1,000,000 or imprisoned not more than 30 years, or both.

–SOURCE–

(Added Pub. L. 98-473, title II, Sec. 1108(a), Oct. 12, 1984, 98 Stat. 2147; amended Pub. L. 101-73, title IX, Sec. 961(k), Aug. 9, 1989, 103 Stat. 500; Pub. L. 101-647, title XXV, Sec. 2504(j), Nov. 29, 1990, 104 Stat. 4861.)

–MISC1–

AMENDMENTS

1990 – Pub. L. 101-647 substituted "30" for "20" before "years".

1989 – Pub. L. 101-73 amended section generally, restating former subsec. (a) and striking out former subsec. (b) which defined "federally chartered or insured financial institution". Prior to amendment, subsec. (a) read as follows: "Whoever knowingly executes, or attempts to execute, a scheme or artifice —

> "(1) to defraud a federally chartered or insured financial institution; or
>
> "(2) to obtain any of the moneys, funds, credits, assets, securities or other property owned by or under the custody or control of a federally chartered or insured financial institution by means of false or fraudulent pretenses, representations, or promises, shall be fined not more than $10,000, or imprisoned not more than five years, or both."

–SECREF–

SECTION REFERRED TO IN OTHER SECTIONS

This section is referred to in sections 225, 981, 982, 1510, 1961, 2326, 3059A, 3293, 3322 of this title; title 12 sections 1785, 1786, 1787, 1821, 1828, 1829, 1831k, 1833a, 2277a-10b.

15 USC Section 1644

–EXPCITE–

TITLE 15 — COMMERCE AND TRADE

CHAPTER 41 — CONSUMER CREDIT PROTECTION

SUBCHAPTER I — CONSUMER CREDIT COST DISCLOSURE

PART B — CREDIT TRANSACTIONS

–HEAD–

Sec. 1644. Fraudulent use of credit cards; penalties

–STATUTE–

(a) Use, attempt or conspiracy to use card in transaction affecting interstate or foreign commerce

Whoever knowingly in a transaction affecting interstate or foreign commerce, uses or attempts or conspires to use any counterfeit, fictitious, altered, forged, lost, stolen, or fraudulently obtained credit card to obtain money, goods, services, or anything else of value which within any one-year period has a value aggregating $1,000 or more; or

(b) Transporting, attempting or conspiring to transport card in interstate commerce

Whoever, with unlawful or fraudulent intent, transports or attempts or conspires to transport in interstate or foreign commerce a counterfeit, fictitious, altered, forged, lost, stolen, or fraudulently obtained credit card knowing the same to be counterfeit, fictitious, altered, forged, lost, stolen, or fraudulently obtained; or

(c) Use of interstate commerce to sell or transport card

Whoever, with unlawful or fraudulent intent, uses any instrumentality of interstate or foreign commerce to sell or transport a counterfeit, fictitious, altered, forged, lost, stolen, or fraudulently obtained credit card knowing the same to be counterfeit, fictitious, altered, forged, lost, stolen, or fraudulently obtained; or

(d) Receipt, concealment, etc., of goods obtained by use of card

Whoever knowingly receives, conceals, uses, or transports money, goods, services, or anything else of value (except tickets for interstate or foreign transportation) which (1) within any one-year period has a value aggregating $1,000 or more, (2) has moved in or is part of, or which constitutes interstate or foreign commerce, and (3) has been obtained with a counterfeit, fictitious, altered, forged, lost, stolen, or fraudulently obtained credit card; or

(e) Receipt, concealment, etc., of tickets for interstate or foreign transportation obtained by use of card

Whoever knowingly receives, conceals, uses, sells, or transports in interstate or foreign commerce one or more tickets for interstate or foreign transportation, which (1) within any one-year period have a value aggregating $500 or more, and (2) have been purchased or obtained with one or more counterfeit, fictitious, altered, forged, lost, stolen, or fraudulently obtained credit cards; or

(f) Furnishing of money, etc., through use of card

Whoever in a transaction affecting interstate or foreign commerce furnishes money, property, services, or anything else of value, which within any one-year period has a value aggregating $1000 or more, through the use of any counterfeit, fictitious, altered, forged, lost, stolen, or fraudulently obtained credit card knowing the same to be counterfeit, fictitious, altered, forged, lost, stolen, or fraudulently obtained —

shall be fined not more than $10,000 or imprisoned not more than ten years, or both.

–SOURCE–

(Pub. L. 90-321, title I, Sec. 134, as added Pub. L. 91-508, title V, Sec. 502(a), Oct. 26, 1970, 84 Stat. 1127; amended Pub. L. 93-495, title IV, Sec. 414, Oct. 28, 1974, 88 Stat. 1520.)

–MISC1–

AMENDMENTS

1974 – Pub. L. 93-495 generally reorganized provisions by designating former unlettered paragraph cls. (a) to (f), and as so designated, expanded prohibitions relating to fraudulent use of credit cards, decreased amount required for fraudulent use from a retail value aggregating $5,000, or more, to enumerated amounts for particular activities, and increased the punishment from a sentence of not more than five years to a sentence of not more than ten years.

EFFECTIVE DATE OF 1974 AMENDMENT

Amendment by Pub. L. 93-495 effective Oct. 28, 1974, see section 416 of Pub. L. 93-495, set out as an Effective Date note under section 1665a of this title.

EFFECTIVE DATE

Section 503(3) of Pub. L. 91-508 provided that: "Section 134 of such Act (this section) applies to offenses committed on or after such date of enactment (Oct. 26, 1970)."

–SECREF–

SECTION REFERRED TO IN OTHER SECTIONS

This section is referred to in section 1645 of this title.

15 USC Section 1693

–EXPCITE–

TITLE 15 — COMMERCE AND TRADE

CHAPTER 41 — CONSUMER CREDIT PROTECTION

SUBCHAPTER VI — ELECTRONIC FUND TRANSFERS

–HEAD–

Sec. 1693. Congressional findings and declaration of purpose

–STATUTE–

(a) Rights and liabilities undefined

The Congress finds that the use of electronic systems to transfer funds provides the potential for substantial benefits to consumers. However, due to the unique characteristics of such systems, the application of existing consumer protection legislation is unclear, leaving the rights and liabilities of consumers, financial institutions, and intermediaries in electronic fund transfers undefined.

(b) Purposes

It is the purpose of this subchapter to provide a basic framework establishing the rights, liabilities, and responsibilities of participants in electronic fund transfer systems. The primary objective of this subchapter, however, is the provision of individual consumer rights.

–SOURCE–

(Pub. L. 90-321, title IX, Sec. 902, as added Pub. L. 95-630, title XX, Sec. 2001, Nov. 10, 1978, 92 Stat. 3728.)

–MISC1–

EFFECTIVE DATE

Section 921 of title IX of Pub. L. 90-321, as added Pub. L. 95-630, title XX, Sec. 2001, Nov. 10, 1978, 92 Stat. 3741, provided that: "This title (enacting this subchapter) takes effect upon the expiration of eighteen months from the date of its enactment (Nov. 10, 1978) except that sections 909 and 911 (sections 1693g, 1693i of this title) take effect upon the expiration of ninety days after the date of enactment."

SHORT TITLE

This subchapter known as the "Electronic Fund Transfer Act", see Short Title note set out under section 1601 of this title.

18 USC Section 510

–EXPCITE–

TITLE 18 — CRIMES AND CRIMINAL PROCEDURE

PART I — CRIMES

CHAPTER 25 — COUNTERFEITING AND FORGERY

–HEAD–

Sec. 510. Forging endorsements on Treasury checks or bonds or securities of the United States

–STATUTE–

(a) Whoever, with intent to defraud —

(1) falsely makes or forges any endorsement or signature on a Treasury check or bond or security of the United States; or

(2) passes, utters, or publishes, or attempts to pass, utter, or publish, any Treasury check or bond or security of the United States bearing a falsely made or forged endorsement or signature; shall be fined under this title or imprisoned not more than ten years, or both.

(b) Whoever, with knowledge that such Treasury check or bond or security of the United States is stolen or bears a falsely made or forged endorsement or signature buys, sells, exchanges, receives, delivers, retains, or conceals any such Treasury check or bond or security of the United States shall be fined under this title or imprisoned not more than ten years, or both.

(c) If the face value of the Treasury check or bond or security of the United States or the aggregate face value, if more than one Treasury check or bond or security of the United States, does not exceed $1,000, in any of the above-mentioned offenses, the penalty shall be a fine of (FOOTNOTE 1) under this title or imprisonment for not more than one year, or both.

(FOOTNOTE 1) So in original. The word "of" probably should not appear.

–SOURCE–

(Added Pub. L. 98-151, Sec. 115(a), Nov. 14, 1983, 97 Stat. 976; amended Pub. L. 101-647, title XXXV, Sec. 3514, Nov. 29, 1990, 104 Stat. 4923; Pub. L. 103-322, title XXXIII, Sec. 330016(1)(H), (L), Sept. 13, 1994, 108 Stat. 2147; Pub. L. 104-294, title VI, Sec. 602(e), 606(b), Oct. 11, 1996, 110 Stat. 3503, 3511.)

–MISC1–

AMENDMENTS

1996 – Subsec. (b). Pub. L. 104-294, Sec. 602(e), struck out "that in fact is stolen or bears a forged or falsely made endorsement or signature" after "bond or security of the United States".

Subsec. (c). Pub. L. 104-294, Sec. 606(b), substituted "$1000" for "$500".

1994 – Subsecs. (a), (b). Pub. L. 103-322, Sec. 330016(1)(L), substituted "fined under this title" for "fined not more than $10,000".

Subsec. (c). Pub. L. 103-322, Sec. 330016(1)(H), substituted "fined under this title" for "fined not more than $1000".

1990 – Subsec. (a). Pub. L. 101-647 inserted semicolon after "or signature" in par. (2) and moved provisions beginning with "shall be fined" flush with left margin.

–SECREF–

SECTION REFERRED TO IN OTHER SECTIONS

This section is referred to in sections 981, 982, 3056 of this title.

18 USC Section 513

–SECREF–

TITLE 18 — CRIMES AND CRIMINAL PROCEDURE

PART I — CRIMES

CHAPTER 25 — COUNTERFEITING AND FORGERY

–HEAD–

Sec. 513. Securities of the States and private entities

–STATUTE–

(a) Whoever makes, utters or possesses a counterfeited security of a State or a political subdivision thereof or of an organization, or whoever makes, utters or possesses a forged security of a State or political subdivision thereof or of an organization, with intent to deceive another person, organization, or government shall be fined under this title (FOOTNOTE 1) or imprisoned for not more than ten years, or both.

(FOOTNOTE 1) See 1994 Amendment note below.

(b) Whoever makes, receives, possesses, sells or otherwise transfers an implement designed for or particularly suited for making a counterfeit or forged security with the intent that it be so used shall be punished by a fine under this title or by imprisonment for not more than ten years, or both.

(c) For purposes of this section —

(1) the term "counterfeited" means a document that purports to be genuine but is not, because it has been falsely made or manufactured in its entirety;

(2) the term "forged" means a document that purports to be genuine but is not because it has been falsely altered, completed, signed, or endorsed, or contains a false addition thereto or insertion therein, or is a combination of parts of two or more genuine documents;

(3) the term "security" means —

(A) a note, stock certificate, treasury stock certificate, bond, treasury bond, debenture, certificate of deposit, interest coupon, bill, check, draft, warrant, debit instrument as defined in section 916(c) of the Electronic Fund Transfer Act, money order, traveler's check, letter of credit, warehouse receipt, negotiable bill of lading, evidence of indebtedness, certificate of interest in or participation in any profit-sharing agreement, collateral-trust certificate, pre-reorganization certificate of subscription, transferable share, investment contract, voting trust certificate, or certificate of interest in tangible or intangible property;

(B) an instrument evidencing ownership of goods, wares, or merchandise;

(C) any other written instrument commonly known as a security;

(D) a certificate of interest in, certificate of participation in, certificate for, receipt for, or warrant or option or other right to subscribe to or purchase, any of the foregoing; or

(E) a blank form of any of the foregoing;

(4) the term "organization" means a legal entity, other than a government, established or organized for any purpose, and includes a corporation, company, association, firm, partnership, joint stock company, foundation, institution, society,

union, or any other association of persons which operates in or the activities of which affect interstate or foreign commerce; and

(5) the term "State" includes a State of the United States, the District of Columbia, Puerto Rico, Guam, the Virgin Islands, and any other territory or possession of the United States.

–SOURCE–

(Added Pub. L. 98-473, title II, Sec. 1105(a), Oct. 12, 1984, 98 Stat. 2144, Sec. 511; renumbered Sec. 513, Pub. L. 99-646, Sec. 31(a), Nov. 10, 1986, 100 Stat. 3598; amended Pub. L. 101-647, title XXXV, Sec. 3515, Nov. 29, 1990, 104 Stat. 4923; Pub. L. 103-322, title XXXIII, Sec. 330008(1), 330016(2)(C), Sept. 13, 1994, 108 Stat. 2142, 2148.)

REFERENCES IN TEXT

Section 916(c) of the Electronic Fund Transfer Act, referred to in par. (3)(A), is classified to section 1693n(c) of Title 15, Commerce and Trade.

–MISC1–

AMENDMENTS

1994 – Subsec. (a). Pub. L. 103-322, Sec. 330016(2)(C), which directed the amendment of this section by substituting "under this title" for "of not more than $250,000", was executed by making the substitution for "not more than $250,000", to reflect the probable intent of Congress.

Subsec. (b). Pub. L. 103-322, Sec. 330016(2)(C), substituted "fine under this title" for "fine of not more than $250,000". Subsec. (c)(4). Pub. L. 103-322, Sec. 330008(1), substituted "association of persons" for "association or persons".

1990 – Subsec. (c)(3)(A). Pub. L. 101-647 struck out "(15 USC 1693(c))" after "Electronic Fund Transfer Act" and inserted comma after "profit-sharing agreement".

–SECREF–

SECTION REFERRED TO IN OTHER SECTIONS

This section is referred to in sections 514, 1956 of this title.

18 USC Section 514

–EXPCITE–

TITLE 18 — CRIMES AND CRIMINAL PROCEDURE

PART I — CRIMES

CHAPTER 25 — COUNTERFEITING AND FORGERY

–HEAD–

Sec. 514. Fictitious obligations

–STATUTE–

(a) Whoever, with the intent to defraud —

(1) draws, prints, processes, produces, publishes, or otherwise makes, or attempts or causes the same, within the United States;

(2) passes, utters, presents, offers, brokers, issues, sells, or attempts or causes the same, or with like intent possesses, within the United States; or

(3) utilizes interstate or foreign commerce, including the use of the mails or wire, radio, or other electronic communication, to transmit, transport, ship, move, transfer, or attempts or causes the same, to, from, or through the United States, any false or fictitious instrument, document, or other item appearing, representing, purporting, or contriving through scheme or artifice, to be an actual security or other financial instrument issued under the authority of the United States, a foreign government, a State or other political subdivision of the United States, or an organization, shall be guilty of a class B felony.

(b) For purposes of this section, any term used in this section that is defined in section 513(c) has the same meaning given such term in section 513(c).

(c) The United States Secret Service, in addition to any other agency having such authority, shall have authority to investigate offenses under this section.

–SOURCE–

(Added Pub. L. 104-208, div. A, title I, Sec. 101(f) (title VI, Sec. 648(b)(1)), title II, Sec. 2603(b)(1), Sept. 30, 1996, 110 Stat. 3009-314, 3009-367, 3009-470.)

–MISC1–

CODIFICATION

Sections 101(f) (title VI, Sec. 648(b)(1)) and 2603(b)(1) of div. A of Pub. L. 104-208 added identical sections 514.

EFFECTIVE DATE

Section effective Sept. 30, 1996, and to remain in effect for each fiscal year following Sept. 30, 1996, see section 101(f) (title VI, Sec. 648(c)) of Pub. L. 104-208, set out as an Effective Date of 1996 Amendment note under section 474 of this title.

Appendix B. Commonly Used Sections of United Kingdom Law

Existing Statutory Conspiracies

Following is a sample of fraud and related laws in the United Kingdom.

Section 5(6)

Section 5(6) effectively retains those conspiracies, with the exception of conspiracy to murder, that already exist under some other enactment (e.g., Conspiracy to Cause and Explosion contrary to Section 3, Explosive Substancces Act 1883). It further states that such an offense will not be an offense contrary to Section I, Criminal Justice Act: 1977, but shall be subject to the same legal interpretation.

Conspiracy To Defraud: Criminal Justice Act 1987

Section 12

(1) "If —

(a) a person agrees with any other person or persons that a course of conduct shall be pursued; and

(b) That course of conduct will necessarily amount to or involve the commission of any offense or offenses by one or more of the parties to the agreement if the agreement is carried out in accordance with their intentions.

The fact that is will do so shall not preclude a charge of conspiracy to defraud being brought against any of them in respect of the agreement."

Penalty: 10 years

For example, a publisher conspires with an employee of a rival publisher to copy the manuscripts of a potentially popular novel. He then proceeds to print and publish the novel before his rival, thus reaping the profits that his rival would have received in the ordinary course of events. The manuscript has not been stolen, but the rival publisher has been defrauded.

Common Law Conspiracies

As mentioned at the beginning of this subject, certain Common Law Conspiracies have been retained. Although the Law Commission has declared its intention of incorporating them into Statute Law, they have been retained in their existing form, as otherwise certain criminal acts would go unpunished.

Forgery

Forgery and Counterfeiting Act 1981

Making a False Instrument

Section 1

(1) "A person is guilty of forgery if he makes a false instrument, with the intention that he or another shall use it to induce somebody to accept it as genuine, and by reason of so accepting it to do or not to do some act to his own or any other person's prejudice"

Penalty: 10 years

The Act does not change the well-established principle: "that an instrument must not only tell a lie, it must tell a lie about itself."

Intention: Whenever it is necessary to prove a specific intent, the provisions of Section 8 or the Criminal Justice Act 1967 will apply.

"A Court or jury in determining whether a person has committed an offence, shall:

(a) not be bound in law to infer that he intended or foresaw a result of his actions by reason only of its being a natural and probable consequence of those actions, but

(b) shall decide whether he did intend or foresee that result, by reference to all the evidence, drawing such inferences from the evidence, as appear proper in the circumstances."

The necessary intention must be in the offender's mind at the time he makes the false instrument for his conduct to amount to forgery.

Section 8

Instrument:

(1) "...instrument" means —

(a) any document, whether of a formal or informal character;

(b) any stamp issued or sold by the Post Office,

(c) any Inland Revenue stamp; and

(d) any disc, tape, soundtrack or other device on or in which information is recorded or stored by mechanical electronic or means.

(2) A "currency note" ... is not an instrument for the purposes of this Part of the Act." In practice, the vast majority of forgeries are of documents and the term "formal" will obviously cover documents like Driving Licenses, Certificates of Births, Deaths or Marriages, Test Certificates, Wills and Statements for use in court proceedings, whereas an "informal" document will include personal letters, bills, accounts, etc.

Document: There is no statutory definition of "document", but *Russell on Crime* defines a document as follows: "Writing in any form on any material which communicates to some person or persons a human statement whether fact or fiction." Russell also states that there is a "Real Test" to be applied to decide whether or not an item is a document. The test is this: "Is it a writing which conveys to the mind of all persons able to read it, the same message as the spoken word?" The positive answer to this will include not only letters, but such things as an engineer's blueprint, engine and chassis numbers, documents in Braille, cheque cards and credit cards. I will exclude such things as paintings, statues and other works of art. It will be realized from this that the material of which the document is made is irrelevant. Thus, a personal cheque written on, for example, a piece of slate, or an article of clothing, will still be a document and therefore an instrument under the Act. It is also clear that the nature of the writing on the document is immaterial (providing the item passes the "Real Test").

Interpretation Act 1889

Section 20

"In this Act, and in every other Act passed before or after the commencement of this Act, expressions referring to writing shall, unless the contrary intention appears, be construed as including reference to printing, lithography, photography, and other modes of presenting or reproducing words in a visual form." Therefore, words will include figures, letters, and symbols.

Stamp Issued or Sold by the Post Office... : The Section makes it apparent that this refers to the adhesive type of stamps sold by the Post Office and not the hand stamps used for franking purposes, although Section 8(3) makes it clear that the mark made by these is capable of being forged. This Section also states that a mark denoting payment of postage which the Post Offices authorises to be used instead of an adhesive stamp is to be included in the term "Stamp" (i.e., Postal Franking Machines). The interpretation is not purely limited to postage stamps but will also include items such as television licence saver stamps, vehicle excise licence stamps, etc.

Inland Revenue Stamp: This includes a stamp impressed by means of a die as well as an adhesive stamp for denoting a duty or fee (i.e., Stamp Duty).

Disc, Tape, Soundtrack... : The inclusion of this paragraph clarifies to some extent old arguments as to whether computer programming tapes, computer storage disks, etc. could be the subject of forgery. It now seems clear that these items are "instruments" and, therefore, forgery of them with the necessary *mens rea* will amount to an offence. The paragraph is clearly aimed at computer-related items, but it may also cover forgery (again, with appropriate *mens rea*) of less obvious objects.

It seems likely that recordings of music, television, videocassettes, etc. will not be amenable to prosecution, as these may properly be described as art forms, and unauthorised copying, etc. should be regarded as copyright infringements, or if sold as originals, the subject of prosecutions under Section 15, Theft Act 1968 or under the provisions of the Trade Descriptions Act 1968.

Section 9: False

(1) "An instrument is false...

- (a) if it purports to have been made in the form in which it is made by a person who did not, in fact, make it in that form; or
- (b) If it purports to have been made in the form in which it is made on the authority of a person who did not, in fact, authorise its making in that form; or
- (c) If it purports to have been made in the form in terms in which it is made by a person who did not, in fact, make it in those terms; or
- (d) If it purports to have been made in the form in terms in which it is made on the authority of a person who did not, in fact, authorize its making in those terms; or
- (e) If it purports to have been altered in any respect on the authority of a person who did not, in fact, authorise the alteration in that respect; or
- (f) If it purports to have been altered in any respect by a person who did not, in fact, alter it in that respect; or
- (g) If it purports to have been made or altered on a date on which, or not a place at which, or otherwise in circumstances in which, it was not, in fact, made or altered, or
- (h) if it purports to have been made or altered by an existing person but he did not, in fact, exist."

The Appeal Court has emphasized that word used in legislation should be given their ordinary everyday meaning.

Form: The dictionary meaning of the word "form" refers to "format", "layout", and "design" and this will cover printer matter such as an application form or cheque bearing or example, a false signature.

Terms: The dictionary meaning of the word "terms" refers to "words", "language employed", and "mode of expression". This would, for example, cover such things as a false character reference.

Person: The word "person" as used in paragraphs (a) to (f) refers solely to existing or living persons. The word "person" in paragraph (h) refers to a person who do not exist whether because they are dead, or because they are invented.

Examples: Consider the following circumstances.

(1) John Smith dies without making a will. His son William makes out and signs a will in his late father's name.

(2) William Smith finds his late father's personalized cheque book and issues cheques which he sign John Smith.

Both instruments purport to have been made by an existing person (i.e., John Smith) who did not, in fact, exist at the time of their making and they are both, therefore, false.

Altered: The word "altered" will not only cover insertions, but also deletions, obliterations, removals, etc. Paragraph (d) and (f) provide that an instrument may be false where any unauthorized alteration in any respect (although in practice this will be a material alteration) has been made.

Example: (A) receives a cheque for £8 as a prize for winning a photographic competition and he inserts a "0" after the 8 and a "Y" after the word "eight". This would have the effect of making the cheque a false instrument, as the insertions were neither made by the person who purports to have made them (i.e., the drawee of the cheque) nor by his authority.

The next provision under paragraph (g) will cater for the situation where an instrument purports to have been made or altered on a date, or at a place, or under circumstances in which, in fact, it was not made or altered. Again, in practice, it will be the materiality of the purported circumstance, which will decide whether or not a prosecution should ensue.

Example: Consider the date (or time) of a postmark on an envelope containing a winning pools coupon. If a Post Office employee were to copy the results onto his coupon, apply an incorrect time and date stamp to the envelope, whereby purporting that it was made prior to that date, the instrument would clearly be false.

Section 9: Making

(2) "A person is to be treated for the purposes of this part of the Act as making a false instrument if he alters an instrument as to make it false in any respect (whether or not it is false in some other respect), apart from that alteration.

This simply provides the "catch-all" subsection whereby an instrument can be regarded as being "false" if it is altered in any way which would not otherwise be covered satisfactorily by the paragraphs (a) to (n) under Section 9(1).

Section 10: Prejudice

(1) "... an act or omission intended to be induced, is to a person's prejudice if, and only if, it is one which if it occurs —

- (a) will result —
  - (i) in his temporary or permanent loss of property; or
  - (ii) in his being deprived of an opportunity to gain a financial advantage otherwise than by way of remuneration; or
- (b) will result in somebody being given an opportunity —
  - (i) to earn remuneration or greater remuneration from him; or
  - (ii) to gain a financial advantage from his otherwise than by way of remuneration; or
- (c) will be the result of his having accepted a false instrument as genuine or a copy of a false instrument as a copy of a genuine one, in connection with his performance of any duty."

The wording of this is fairly straightforward. However, the provisions under (a)(ii) might be more easily understood if the following is considered.

Example: Smith and Jones are teachers. Both apply for a teaching post at another school. Smith is poorly qualify, but Jones is an admirable suitable candidate. Whilst in the school secretary's office, Smith sees a character reference for Jones from their present Headmaster. Smith alters some of the report which as a result then decries Jones as a candidate. The report is sent by post and is in due course considered by the prospective employer, who, as a result of the alterations, decides not to employ Jones. In that case the "omission" to employ would be to Jones' "prejudice" under (a)(ii) above. If Smith altered his own poor report to one which then became a glowing testimonial and as a result he was employed, then the "act" of employing would be to the employer's "prejudice" by virtue of the provision (b)(i).

A similar situation under paragraphs (a)(ii) would exist if, instead of the chance of employment in the above example being the "prejudicial act or omission" one replaces this with the chance to win money, perhaps by opening a credit account at a betting office. It will be noticed that these provisions are to some degree compatible with those under Section 16, Theft Act 1968. The remaining paragraph (c) is probably best illustrated by the circumstances of a decided case under the Forgery Act 1913.

R v Garland (1960)

An off-duty police officer, who was a learner driver, was involved in an accident and was not displaying "L" plates or accompanied by a competent driver. When asked by police for his driving license, he pretended he did not have it with him and arranged to produce it at his own station later. The completed form HORT-2 was put in error in his own pigeon-hole at his station, and he filled it in as if a correct driving license had been produced and signed his inspector's signature on the form HORT-2, then sent it back to the originating Police Station. As a result, no proceedings were started against him for Road Traffic offences.

Held: "There was no difference in law between causing persons to refrain from acting. In causing the police to refrain from performing their duty he was inducing them to act to their injury and to the injury of the public".

(2) "An act which a person has enforceable duty to do, and an omission to an act which a person is not entitled to do shall be disregarded for the purposes of the Part of the Act."

In simple English, this means if, as a result of someone accepting a false instrument (or a copy of one) as genuine, that person is induced to do some act which he has an enforceable duty to do then the doing of the act is not regarded as being to his "prejudice". Similarly, if one is induced by accepting a false instrument, etc. to refrain from doing an act which one is not entitled to do, then that "omission" is not regarded as being to one's "prejudice".

Section 10: Induce

(3) "In this Part of the Act references to inducing somebody to accept a false instrument as genuine, or a copy of a false instrument as a copy of a genuine one, include references to inducing a machine to respond to the instrument or copy as if it were a genuine instrument or, as the case may be, a copy of a genuine one."

(4) "Where subsection (3) above applies, the act or omission intended to be induced by the machine responding to the instrument or copy shall be treated as an act or omission to a person's prejudice."

(5) "In this Section, "loss" includes not getting what one might get as well as parting with what one has..."

Copying a False Instrument

Section 2

"It is an offence for a person to make a copy of an instrument which is, and which he knows or believes to be, a false instrument with the intention that he or another shall use it to induce somebody to accept it as a copy of a genuine instrument, and by reason of so accepting it to do or not to do some act to his own or any other person's prejudice."

Penalty: 10 years

As under Section 1, this offence is complete as soon as a person makes the copy of false instrument (with the necessary knowledge or belief, and intention).

Example: Smith and Jones are not criminals. Smith suggests they can make money for themselves by acting as authorised collectors for a charity. In order to induce householders into making donations, Smith prints a form of authorisation which falsely purports to be signed by the president of a well-known charity. So that Jones can also engage in the fraudulent collection, he photostats the "authorisation".

It is important to note that Section 2 does not concern itself with the copying of genuine instruments. It is concerned with the copies of forged instruments only.

Using a False Instrument

Section 3

"It is an offence for a person to use an instrument which is, and which he knows or believes to be, false with the intention of inducing somebody to accept it as genuine and by reason of so accepting it to do or not to do some act to his own or any other person's prejudice."

Penalty: 10 years

Using a Copy of a False Instrument

Section 4

"It is an offence for a person to use a copy of an instrument which is, and which he knows or believes to be, a false instrument with the intention of inducing somebody to accept it as a copy of a genuine instrument, and by reason of so accepting it to do or not to do some act to his own or another person's prejudice."

Penalty: 10 years

Use: The offence of "using" replaces the old crime of "uttering" by using "is believed" to encompass the same activities as the former term. In simple terms, it seems that to make any use whatsoever of the false instrument or copy, with the necessary *mens rea*, will amount to an offence.

R v Harris (1966) 129 JPP 5542

The important word in the definition of "utter" in Section 6(2) is the word "uses" which has a very wide meaning. In this case, (H) falsely pretended that he had paid a debt due to (S) and in support of that pretence he produced a forged receipt purporting to bear the signature of an agent of (S) and had a photostat copy made by his solicitor and sent the cop to (S) with the intent to defraud.

Held: There had been a "use" by the appellant of the forged receipt within the meaning of Section 6(2) and rightly convicted of "uttering".

R v Finkelstein (1886)

Appellants contended that the posting of forged documents did not constitute an uttering until those forged documents were received and opened by the addressee.

Held: The posting of forged bonds in London to a company in Brussels constituted an uttering of the bonds in London (*R v Giles 1827* followed).

R v Tobierre (1986) All ER 346

The prosecution must prove a double intention:

(1) to induce someone to accept an instrument as genuine: and

(2) that the other person should act or omit to act to his own or someone else's prejudice.

The offences contained in Sections 1 to 4 cover the making and use of any false instrument (or copying and use). The Act of 1981 makes no distinction between Public or Private instruments and the *mens rea* required in all cases in the same.

Possession of Certain "Specified" False Instruments

Specified instruments: The Legislators realised that the mere existence when forged of certain instruments poses such a serious threat as to justify the prohibition of possession both of the instruments and of the immediate materials for making them.

Section 5

(1) "It is an offence for a person to have in his custody or under his control an instrument to which this Section applies which is, and which he knows or believes to be, false with the intention that he or another shall use it to induce somebody to accept it as genuine, and by reason of so accepting it to do or not to do some act to his own or any other person's prejudice."

(2) "It is an offence for a person to have in his custody or under his control, without lawful authority or excuse, an instrument to which this Section applies which is, and which he knows or believes to be, false."

The offences under subsections (1) and (2) both relate to having "custody or control" of any "specified" false instrument. The offences differ only in the *mens rea* of the offender (i.e., the offence under subsection (1) provides for the person who has the false instrument with intent to use, etc., whereas a person will offend against subsection (2) when he has the instrument "without lawful authority or excuse").

(3) "It is an offence for a person to make or to have in his custody or under his control a machine or implements or paper or any other material which to his

knowledge is or has been specifically designed or adapted for the making of an instrument to which this Section applies, with the intention that he or another shall make an instrument to which this Section applies which is false and that he or another shall use the instrument to induce somebody to accept it as genuine, and by reason of so accepting it to do or not to do some act to his own or any other person's prejudice."

(4) "It is an offence for a person to make or to have in his custody or under his control any such machine, implement, paper or material, without lawful authority or excuse."

The offences under subsections (3) and (4) are separated in exactly the same way with respect to the *mens rea* involved. However, these subsections are directed against "making" or "custody or control" of items used for making any of the "specified" false instruments.

In his custody or under his control: This has a far wider meaning than mere "possession". It seems probable that if Jones were to store implements, etc. for making one of the specified instruments in a room at the rear of a friend's business premises, Jones would still have effective "control" of them.

Instrument: Subsection (5) lists the specified false instruments to which all the offences under Section 5 relate:

(a) Money orders;

(b) Postal orders;

(c) United Kingdom postage stamps;

(d) Inland revenue stamps;

(e) Share certificates;

(f) Passports and documents which can be used instead of passports;

(g) Cheques;

(h) Travellers' cheques;

(i) Cheque cards;

(j) Credit cards;

(k) Certified copies relating to an entry in a register of births, adoptions, marriages, or deaths and issued by the Registrar General, the Registrar General for Northern Ireland, a registration officer, or a person lawfully authorised to register marriages; and

(l) Certificates relating to entries in such registers

(6) "Share certificates" means an instrument entitling or evidencing the title of a person to a share or interest —

(a) "In any public stock, annuity fund or debt of any government of state, including a state which forms part of another state which forms part of another state; or

(b) in any stock, fund or debt or a body (whether corporate or unincorporated) established in the United Kingdom or elsewhere."

Punishment: Triable either way. The punishments on indictment, however, vary according to the *mens rea* of the possessor, as follows.

- Subsection (1) and (3) offences on indictment — imprisonment not exceeding 10 years.
- Subsection (2) and (4) offences on indictment — imprisonment not exceeding 2 years.

Police Powers

In respect to Sections (5) number (2) and (4) "General Arrest Conditions" under PACE 1984 apply.

Director of Public Prosecutions

Certain offences under the Forgery and Counterfeiting Act 1981 have to be made subject of a report to the DPP by virtue of the Prosecution of Offences Regulations 1978. The relevant offences under Part 1 of the Act are: "Offences under Sections 1 to 4 of the Forgery and Counterfeiting Act 1981 concerning document of a type specified in Section 2(1)(a) and (b) and Section 3 the Forgery Act 1913 and of seals and dies of a type specified in Section 5 of the (1913) Act." These will include forgery of wills, bonds, assignments, deeds, documents bearing impressions of public seals etc. and registers or copies of registers relating to birth, deaths, marriages, etc.

Powers of Search and Forfeiture

Section 7

(1) "If it appears to a justice of the peace, from information given him on oath, that there is reasonable cause to believe that a person has in his custody or under his control —

(a) Anything which he or another has used, whether before or after the coming into force of this Act, or intend to use, for the making of any false instrument or copy of a false instrument, in contravention of Section 1 or 2 above; or

(b) Any false instrument or copy of a false instrument which he or another has used, whether before or after the coming into force of this Act, or intends to use, in contravention of Section 3 or 4 above; or

(c) Anything custody or control of which without lawful authority or excuse is an offence under Section 5 above;

(2) "A Constable may at any time after the seizure of any object suspected of falling within paragraph (a), (b) or (c) of subsection (1) above (whether the seizure was effected by virtue of a warrant under that subsection or otherwise) apply to a Magistrates' Court for an order under this subsection with respect to the object; and the court, if it is satisfied both that the object, in fact, falls within any of those paragraphs and that it is conductive to the public interest to do so, may make such order as its thinks fit for the forfeiture of the object and its subsequent destruction or disposal."

(3) "Subject to subsection (4) below, the court by or before which a person is convicted of an offence under this part of the Act may order any object shown to the satisfaction of the court to relate to the offence to be forfeited and either destroyed or dealt within such other manner as the court may order."

(4) "The court shall not order any object to be forfeited under subsection (2) or (3) above where a person claiming to be the owner of or otherwise interest in it applies to be heard by the court, unless an opportunity has been given to him to show case why the order should not be made."

Criminal Procedure Act 1965

Section 8

Comparison of a disputed writing with any writing proved to the satisfaction of the judge to be genuine shall be permitted to be made by witnesses, and such writing and evidence of witnesses respecting the same may be submitted to the Court and jury as evidence of genuineness or otherwise of the writing in dispute.

Appendix C. Nigerian Advance Fee Fraud Prevention Act

Nigerian Advance Fee Fraud Prevention Act of 1998 (Introduced in the House) HR 3916 IH

Following is a sample of a Bill introduced by the U.S. House of Representatives (H.R. 3916) — Reference Nigerian Advance Fee Fraud

105th Congress

2d Session

H.R. 3916

Expressing the sense of the Congress regarding the need to address Nigerian advance fee fraud, and for other purposes.

IN THE HOUSE OF REPRESENTATIVES

May 20, 1998

Mr. MARKEY (for himself Mr. ROYCE, Mr. PAYNE, Mr. CAMPBELL, Mr. MENENDEZ, Mr. McDADE, Ms. McKINNEY, Mr. BARRETT of Nebraska, Mr. SCHUMER, Mr. LATOURETTE, Mr. McGOVERN, Mr. METCALF, Mr. STARK, Ms. RIVERS, Mr. HOLDEN, and Ms. FURSE) introduced the following bill, which was referred to the Committee on International Relations.

A BILL

Expressing the sense of the Congress regarding the need to address Nigerian advance fee fraud, and for other purposes.

Be it enacted by the Senate and House of Representatives of the United States of America in Congress assembled,

Section 1. Short Title

This Act may be cited as the 'Nigerian Advance Fee Fraud Prevention Act of 1998'.

Section 2. Findings

The Congress makes the following findings:

(1) Nigerian advance fee fraud, known internationally as "4-1-9" fraud after the section of the Nigerian penal code which addresses fraud schemes, has reached epidemic proportions.

(2) Such frauds generally involve a company or individual that receives an unsolicited letter from a Nigerian claiming to be a senior civil servant of the Nigerian Government, usually from the Nigerian National Petroleum Corporation.

(3) The Nigerian perpetrator of the fraud explains that the entity of the Nigerian Government concerned is seeking a reputable foreign company or individual to use its account to deposit funds ranging from $10,000,000 to $60,000,000, which the Nigerian Government overpaid on a contract.

(4) The intended victims of such frauds are typically asked to provide company letterhead and bank account information which they are told will be used to show completion of the contract.

(5) The victim's letterhead is actually used to forge letters to other prospective victims and to forge letters of recommendation for travel visas from the United States Embassy in Lagos, Nigeria.

(6) Victims of such frauds are pressured to send money for unforeseen taxes, fees to the Nigerian Government, and attorney fees.

(7) Victims of such frauds are requested to travel to Nigeria to complete the fraudulent transaction, and are told a visa is not necessary to enter the country.

(8) The perpetrators of such frauds often bribe airport officials to bypass a victim of such fraud through immigration, and use the victim's illegal entry into the country as leverage to coerce the victim into releasing more funds to the perpetrators.

(9) Violence and threats of physical harm have also been used to pressure victims of such frauds.

(10) 15 foreign businessmen, including 2 United States citizens, have been murdered after traveling to Nigeria in pursuit of a 4-1-9 scam.

(11) Financial losses incurred by United States citizens and reported to the United States Secret Service exceed $100,000,000.

(12) The money derived from these schemes is often used to fund other illegal activities, including drug trafficking and violent crimes.

(13) The United States Secret Service has established 'Operation 4-1-9', which is designed to target these schemes, and the Secret Service receives over 100 telephone calls and 300 to 500 pieces of mail from victims of such schemes every day.

(14) Perpetrators of 4-1-9 frauds are rarely prosecuted or jailed by the Nigerian Government, and money lost is rarely recovered.

(15) The Nigerian Government is suspected of playing a role in these schemes, at least insofar as it has not made any serious efforts to curb the schemes, enforce its own laws against the schemes, or apprehend and prosecute the perpetrators.

Section 3. Efforts To End the Nigerian Advance Fee Fraud

(a) **Sense of Congress:** It is the sense of the Congress that —

(1) the United States should work with the international community to ensure the prosecution of Nigerian scam artists involved in the advance fee frauds described in section 2; and

(2) the United States should take all steps necessary to educate the public about such advance fee fraud, and to prevent future occurrences of such fraud.

(b) **Reports to Congress:** Not later than 1 year after the date of the enactment of this Act, the Secretary of State and the Secretary of the Treasury shall jointly submit to the Congress a report which includes the following information:

(1) Actions undertaken by the Nigerian Government to cooperate with international officials in apprehending and extraditing persons responsible for committing advance fee fraud described in section 2 and preventing future occurrences of such fraud.

(2) Efforts undertaken to inform United States citizens about such advance fee fraud.

(3) Efforts undertaken to ensure the coordination of activities by the United States Government relating to such fraud.

(4) Efforts undertaken to work with the international community to combat such fraud and apprehend the perpetrators.

(5) Other measures being undertaken, and which will be undertaken, to ensure and promote an end to such advance fee fraud, including the imposition of economic and other sanctions on the Government of Nigeria.

Index

Index

D

E

T

U

V

W